He who digs a hole for another may fall in himself.

Russian proverb.

John Burkett RIBA, AADIPL, FCIARB

John Burkett has been a principal in private practice for over thirty years during which time he has received a number of awards, including the Financial Times Award in 1971. He is now a consultant on contractual matters and is the Royal Institute of British Architects (RIBA) Adviser on Conciliation and joint author of the RIBA and Association of Consultant Architects (ACA) conciliation procedures. He is an accredited mediator and has been a member of the Council of the ACA. He represents the ACA on the Construction Industry Council (CIC) Industry Practice Committee where he has been chairman of the Disputes Resolution and Adjudication Task Forces. He is currently a member of the CIC Liability Task Force and of the Forum for Construction Law Reform.

CONTENTS

Acknowledgements

This book would not have been possible without contributions from various sources, which I have listed in the bibliography and for which I am most grateful.

I am also indebted to the Centre for Dispute Resolution (CEDR) for their excellent courses on the techniques of mediation. I have quoted extensively from Sir Michael Latham's report of 1994, *Constructing the Team,* that remains a definitive and far-seeing document on the reforms required in the construction industry.

Where possible I have made specific acknowledgements in the text to individuals, organisations, publications and quotations, each of which have been provided with a note in the text referring to their source. Mark Lane has been particularly helpful with his tactful advice while a special thanks is due to my wife Noel Wurr for her advice and for correcting my spelling and punctuation.

FOREWORD

This is a timely publication.

Some ten years ago alternative dispute resolution (ADR) first began to be talked about seriously in this country and practising disputes lawyers were offered a different way of approaching their subject – the change was from rights-based solutions to interest-based solutions.

It is not really surprising that in a traditional culture like ours, it has taken some time for this initial seed to grow, but most people today agree that ADR's time has come.

The single most important contributor to this sea change is, as John Burkett points out in this book, the reforms introduced last year to our court procedures by Lord Woolf.

Lord Woolf was very much influenced by the civil justice systems of the United States, Australia and Germany. Case management in those jurisdictions is coupled with systems of ADR which the courts can insist that the parties should follow. Under our own new Civil Procedure Rules the court is empowered to stay court proceedings of its own initiative in order to enable ADR to be attempted even if the parties are against it.

Now that ADR in its various forms has been embraced by the Civil Procedure Rules and by the judges themselves, it is possible that litigation itself in the 21st century will eventually become the alternative method of dispute resolution as mediation, conciliation and similar procedures filter out a large proportion of disputes that would in former times have been processed by litigation.

Indeed many mediations now take place because the parties' legal advisers believe that if they go to law the courts will pressure them to mediate in any event. So they may as well try the process of their own volition.

The object of this book is to introduce architects and other consultants to the new world of ADR and the changes it is bringing about not only to methods of dispute resolution, but also to the forms of contract and the way that members of the project team relate to each other.

One of the interesting features of this new world is the obvious preference disputing parties have when selecting mediators for individuals who understand their own industries and backgrounds. This seems particularly true of the construction industry, in spite of the advice constantly offered by the ADR service providers that what really matters is not industry expertise, but true mediation skills.

Consultants in the construction industry are therefore uniquely placed, by virtue of their training and experience, to respond to this need and to offer user-friendly problem solving skills to projects both large and small. This book offers a comprehensive introduction to this brave new world for hard-pressed practitioners with little time or inclination to read the heavyweight volumes on ADR to be found in legal libraries.

The author is well placed to help this process, having enjoyed a distinguished career as an architect before devoting time to contractual and contentious issues with such bodies as the RIBA, the ACA and the CIC. Step by step he takes the reader through the maze of new terminology that we all have to get used to these days. Most readers with experience of new statutory adjudication will agree that this procedure is not conducive to fostering good relationships during projects, and that the right time to think about better ways of handling disputes is at the beginning of the job before difficulties have arisen.

It is fair to say that ADR is closely connected with the growth of partnering in construction. Although this concept is still being explored in the context of our standard form contracts, it inevitably leads to methods of dispute resolution with more than a hint of ADR about them.

Partnering charters typically require the involvement of senior executives of the parties at the very early stages of conflicts. Mediators or Dispute Review Boards are seen as the preferred solution if an independent presence becomes essential.

Disputes without Tears draws these threads together in a very accessible fashion. This book deserves a wide audience and makes a valuable contribution to our contemporary dialogue about the relationship between contracts and dispute resolution.

I commend it heartily.

Tony Blackler
Macfarlanes Solicitors
April 2000

PREFACE

The purpose of this book is to encourage architects and other construction consultants to take a more active role in the selection of forms of agreement and particularly in the methods of settling disputes that have become the bane of the construction industry. Over the years there has been a gradual erosion of the independence of the architect or engineer. It used to be thought that they operated in a quasi-arbitral capacity free of liability. This is now recognised as incorrect but the duty to act fairly between the parties remains.

As a result it is becoming more and more difficult for architects and other consultants to take an independent view as, in spite of this duty to act fairly, they remain the agents of the client and are continuously at risk from pressures both from the client and the contractor. Many of the decisions they have to make may be controversial and in order to avoid disputes it would be helpful if the parties were able to refer the matter elsewhere for a truly independent opinion before embarking on the usual confrontational methods of resolving disputes.

There is now evidence that we are moving away from the traditional adversarial culture and towards a more co-operative attitude where the progress and the satisfactory completion of a project is the primary objective rather than using it as the means by which the maximum profit can be extracted. As always, the lawyers and other experts are jumping on this new 'bandwagon' and already there are several books published on various methods of dispute resolution with more to come. The judiciary, insurers and various commercial interests are realising that too much time, energy and money is being spent on complex and interminable disputes when all that may be wanted is a reasonable financial settlement. Professional Indemnity Insurers consider that of the money paid out in construction cases more than fifty per cent is accounted for by costs rather than by compensation.

This book, therefore, is a guide as to what alternative

methods of dispute resolution are available and how they might be incorporated into forms of agreement in the hope that architects in particular will take a more active role in selecting the most appropriate form of contract and method of dispute resolution, and not simply leave it to others who usually carry nothing like the same responsibility or interest in the realisation of a design.

Lord Donaldson is reported as saying:

I cannot imagine a (civil engineering) contract, particularly one of any size, which does not give rise to some disputes. This is not to the discredit of either party to the contract. It is simply the nature of the beast. What is to their discredit is if they fail to resolve those disputes as quickly, economically, and as sensibly as possible. [1]

TERMINOLOGY

Although I have tried to avoid technical terms it is inevitable when writing about legal matters that some jargon will creep in, which I have defined as far as possible where it occurs. There are a number of terms which appear more than once. 'ADR' is generally used to describe various methods of dispute resolution other than litigation. A 'caucus' is a term that has been adopted by various organisations to describe a private meeting between an independent facilitator and one of the parties to a dispute. The 'HGCR Act' refers to the Housing Grants, Construction and Regeneration Act of 1996, while well-known organisations are referred to by their initials. 'Discovery' is the legal term usually applied to the production of documents – it is now superseded by the term 'disclosure'.

1   INTRODUCTION

In the heady atmosphere of architectural design the actual process of realising that design, particularly in some architectural schools, is not given sufficient emphasis. It is no good creating a brilliant design if you are ill-equipped to see it through to fruition. The process of design is often seen as separate from the professional obligations of an architect that are relegated to Part III of the examinations instead of being incorporated into the design process from the start. Obvious examples are means of escape and health and safety considerations, both of which are universally applicable to the design of buildings.

The practice of architecture does not finish at the drawing board or on computer-assisted design (CAD). To achieve a satisfactory building it requires not only an accurate specification and working drawings but also a careful follow-through of the construction process, with all its administrative problems and scope for disagreements, before you can be content that the completed building is the one that you designed. Most architects will have experienced with pleasure the occasional contract where the client, contractor and construction consultants have all worked harmoniously as a team, but such an experience is becoming rare. It is time to reverse this trend.

Forms of contract, an essential ingredient in the process, are multiplying and becoming more and more complex. There are at least a dozen versions of the Joint Contracts Tribunal (JCT) Ltd contract ranging from *JCT98* with all its variations to the minor works *Agreement MW98*, plus a whole sheaf of amendments and sub-contract forms (Appendix A). The difficulty with so many variations is that the individual forms may include clauses which although superficially very similar are, in fact, sufficiently different to result in wrong assumptions. This has not been helped by the latest revisions, some of which are confusing or ambiguous.

It is not easy for an architect to decide which form is

the most appropriate, let alone attempt to understand the content. The short answer, I fear, is that many architects do not try to understand and tend to leave it to others to advise or to decide. This is a dangerous practice and it is becoming apparent that many adjudications under the new Housing Grants, Construction and Regeneration (HGCR) Act of 1996 [2] arise simply because architects do not know how to apply the conditions of a building agreement. Ideally what is needed is a single form of contract with alternative options which can be familiar to all parties and which includes, above all, an inexpensive method for resolving disputes as and when they arise.

The second edition of the *New Engineering Contract* (November 1995) [3] goes some way towards achieving this by including some twenty-one optional clauses within the same document. The *ACA Contract* also includes a number of options within the same document, but these are less comprehensive. [4]

Too often current management techniques are based on an adversarial culture where participants are expected to perform solely in the interests of their organisation. Quality often becomes secondary and is left to the much undervalued site agent. Management involving human values seems to be a thing of the past so that now in the year 2000 we are so hedged about by Regulations, Acts of Parliament and complex forms of agreement that there is ample room for human error which is seldom, if ever, deliberate. We look around for whom to blame instead of investigating why the error occurred and seeing how best it can be overcome at the least possible cost.

Particularly when work is scarce, some quite reputable contractors have been tempted to submit a very low tender with the deliberate policy of making up any shortfall with a constant barrage of claims in the hope that some will be successful. As a result, instead of progressing the work, every site meeting may be taken up with arguments about additional costs for one reason or another. The lowest tender should never be accepted without a rigorous examination of the pricing.

These facts have encouraged a whole industry of claim making and associated litigation to the point where the purpose of the construction has almost become secondary. For a client, architect and contractor a building agreement should be a tool in the process of realising a design, only to be referred to when there are serious disagreements. For a claims consultant it appears to be an end in itself to be manipulated regardless of its real purpose; sometimes labelled 'opportunist behaviour'. As a result the whole process has become increasingly adversarial, resulting in the use of carefully worded contracts, standard or bespoke, designed to ensure that the party with the weakest bargaining power is made responsible for as much as possible, leaving the architect in the middle to pick up responsibilities which cannot be apportioned elsewhere.

Thus it continues in spite of Sir Michael Latham's observation . . . *that the industry has become extremely adversarial and that we are paying the price.*[5] Few, other than lawyers, understand the various clauses contained in agreements and those who do differ in their interpretation, producing endless scope for argument and disputes. The traditional remedies are long and expensive and, what seems absurd, are often settled before the completion of an arbitration or on the steps of the court.

Why then could they not be settled much earlier?

Lawyers will argue that it is necessary to explore and verify all the facts, but more often than not this is a process of weeding out inflated claims before arriving at the real substance of the dispute. With the slow process of producing details of claims, replies, requests for further information and reports, it is not surprising that costs escalate and that settlements are sometimes delayed for years.

Unfortunately arbitration has tended to go down the same path where lawyers often use legal arguments to obscure the weaknesses of their client's case. The arbitrator, although under the 1996 Act now has greater powers, may not be sufficiently experienced or courageous to curtail such arguments and finds him/herself intimidated. Lengthy arbitrations or litigation only add to costs so that the whole process has become a lottery where, in some quarters, a mere thirty-five per cent success in a claim is considered satisfactory. Lawyers think differently from architects; they are only involved when things go wrong and, within reason, it does not much matter how long it takes to resolve the issues. Any sensible architect should be concerned that things should progress smoothly and that there should be no delays.

Traditionally the methods of resolving disputes have been by arbitration or by legal proceedings, usually only dealt with after the completion of the contract. The late Lord Denning, who never pulled any punches, is quoted as saying:

Resolving disputes by litigation is frequently lengthy and expensive. Arbitration in the construction context is often as bad or worse.

The introduction of the statutory right to adjudication has enabled disputes to be dealt within a much shorter time scale but it has its disadvantages.

2 ADJUDICATION

The inclusion of the right to adjudication in the Housing Grants, Construction and Regeneration (HGCR) Act of 1996 was the result of Sir Michael Latham's recommendation to produce a swift solution to the problem of disputes and, in particular, the question of cash flow. He states that:

. . . most disputes on site are, I believe, better resolved by speedy decision, i.e. adjudication rather than by a mediation procedure in which the parties reach their own settlement. [6]

In one sense he was accepting the *status quo* by short-circuiting the normal adversarial process while setting aside the disadvantages of adjudication where, except for the less complex cases, there is insufficient time to investigate the full facts which may, therefore, result in 'rough justice'. In the process, as interpreted by the HGCR Act of 1996, there is also the risk of ambush in that the referring party may have ample opportunity to prepare its case, leaving the other party little time to respond. Admittedly, the dispute can be referred to arbitration or litigation but this defeats the object of reaching a rapid settlement while leaving one or other of the parties – or both – dissatisfied and the dispute unresolved.

Another disadvantage of adjudication under the HGCR Act of 1996 is that the adjudicator must take account of both the facts and the law. This precludes any consideration of a purely commercial settlement where the legal rights and wrongs may get in the way of what may only be the need for a financial compromise. This is a situation where the parties might otherwise be able to agree, taking into account various considerations such as the maintenance of good relations and the satisfactory progress of the project. The main advantage of adjudication is that it discourages the withholding of payment for spurious reasons, although even this has its risks in that moneys incorrectly awarded may be difficult to recover if the adjudicator's decision is reversed or modified by subsequent arbitration or litigation.

At best adjudication is a temporary solution not conducive to fostering good relationships. The HGCR Act of 1996 makes it impossible to exclude the right to adjudication in any construction contract except under special circumstances that are expressly stated in the Act. Adjudication applies to any 'difference' or 'dispute' – terms that can be widely interpreted. The Act does not apply to contracts where the employer is a residential occupier. [7] This is an unfortunate omission as it is in these circumstances that many disputes arise and where neither party is sure of its ground. The JCT is intending to remedy this situation by the introduction of a simple form of contract designed for consumers where no consultant is employed. It includes an adjudication clause.

The Institution of Civil Engineers' (ICE) *Conditions of Contract* (Amendment to the Sixth Edition) [8] includes an ingenious arrangement whereby a prerequisite to a difference or dispute is that any 'matter of dissatisfaction' must first be referred to the supervising engineer who must give his decision in writing within one month of the reference. If either party is then dissatisfied with the engineer's decision the 'matter of dissatisfaction' becomes a dispute or difference within the meaning of the HGCR Act of 1996 and can either be referred to adjudication or to conciliation in accordance with the ICE conciliation procedure. So far this has not been challenged but one can foresee legal arguments as to the definition of a 'matter of dissatisfaction' and whether or not it, in fact, constitutes a dispute or difference under the HGCR Act of 1996.

A similar arrangement to the ICE contract exists in the *New Engineering Contract* by the introduction of an 'early warning' clause where the parties are required to attend a meeting as soon as it becomes apparent that there is a problem. The purpose is to try to resolve any matters by negotiation before they become a difference or dispute within the meaning of the HGCR Act of 1996. [9] The rules for adjudication published by the Centre for Dispute Resolution (CEDR) include the option to suspend the proceedings and to refer the matter to mediation. [10]

On the plus side, since the introduction of adjudication, some adjudicators are finding that their role can change to that of adviser, where, by clarifying the issues, the parties agree to settle. It indicates that the parties may prefer, where possible, some form of a negotiated settlement.

Sir Michael Latham quotes from the USA experience:

During the past 50 years much of the United States construction environment has been degraded from one of a positive relationship between all members of the project team to a contest consumed in fault finding and defensiveness which results in litigation. The industry has become extremely adversarial and we are paying the price . . . if the construction industry is to become less adversarial, we must examine the construction process . . . Disputes will continue as long as people fail to trust one another. [11]

3 PARTNERING

Following Sir Michael Latham's report, the Construction Industry Board (CIB) set up a series of working groups to further his recommendations. Working Group 12 published a report in 1997 entitled *Partnering in the Team.* [12] This report was developed further by the CIB in their *Construction Best Practice Programme.*

In 1998 the Egan Report was published [13] recommending a system of partnering particularly between contractors and suppliers, although it also identifies the traditional separation between the design professions and the construction process as a barrier to improvement in the industry. The report also advocates the sharing of saving schemes and an 'open book' policy.

One of the weaknesses of the report is that many of the recommendations depend on an experienced client and a continuous programme of construction. Paragraph 88 states that it is at a loss when it comes to considering the occasional client, a situation that must form the majority of construction projects. Since this report, Nissan, who was cited as an example of imaginative practice, has off-loaded some of its suppliers because of a downturn in its market. This is precisely the problem that periodically faces the construction industry whether it is related to a continuous programme or to a one-off project. What the report has done is to encourage the industry to examine its procedures in a more positive light and has lead to the demonstration projects under the Government M4I scheme.

In partnering, the various parties need to recognise that each member of the team has different aspirations and objectives. The client requires a construction that is fit for its purpose, and which will be delivered on time to an agreed budget. The consultant may wish to demonstrate his skills at a reasonable fee that will also enable him to fulfill his/her duties conscientiously. The contractor, sub-contractors and suppliers will expect clear drawings and instructions which, above all, will be free from variations or changes of mind during the course of construction.

The concept of partnering is really a return to a situation where professionals and contractors worked as a team: a situation which still exists on some smaller contracts, particularly in the regions. The problem lies in the larger contracts which involve more complex technology and a greater number of sub-contractors and suppliers than in the past. Part of the trouble is that directors of building firms are too remote from the actual process of construction and are more concerned with balance sheets. This has led to the proliferation of in-house forms of sub-contract unrelated to the main contract and, frequently, to delays in payments. Another problem is that some clients believe that quality can be enforced entirely through specification without taking into account the effect of price. You cannot obtain a Rolls Royce for the cost of a Ford.

The CIB report, *Partnering in the Team,* defines partnering as:

. . . a management approach used by two or more organisations to achieve specific business objectives by maximising the effectiveness of each participant's resources. The approach is based on mutual objectives, an agreed method of problem resolution, and an active search for continuous measurable improvements . . .

In chapter two it continues:

Partnering is about people and relationships. Cynicism and lack of commitment by a few (particularly at senior level) will destroy the efforts of many. [14]

The CIC Partnering Task Force has identified the development of relationships as one of the most important ingredients of partnering. The late Lord Denning is quoted as saying:

Cash flow is the life-blood of the construction industry. It might be added that when the circulation is impeded by clots the consequence is thrombosis.

How then are we to foster partnering between the members of the project team?

A good illustration of what should not happen is provided by the video, *The Benefit of Foresight*, published by the Construction Industry Council (CIC).[15] Although it concerns a *post mortem* following an accident on a building site not caused directly by any one member of the team, it pinpoints the problems which can arise through lack of co-ordination and an anxiety by the client to get the project started. The moral of this video is closer co-operation and much more careful preplanning.

With partnering, in addition to signing the usual forms of agreement, the parties also sign a supplementary 'Partnering Declaration'. Certain preliminary procedures are necessary:

- The tender and contract documents should state that a Partnering Declaration will be included.

- All relevant parties should sign the Declaration including the principal domestic and nominated sub-contractors and suppliers.

- The principal executives and those who are to be directly involved with the project should attend a preliminary meeting to discuss and decide on procedures before work is started.

This meeting should preferably be conducted in a relaxed environment so that the participants get to know one another rather than dealing with faceless persons at the other end of a telephone or an electronic keyboard. How often these days are we faced with a menu which passes from one person to another, none of whom have any real interest in the problem let alone are able to provide or even care about the answer?

The extent to which the meeting is informal or structured very much depends on the size and complexity of the project. However, the project leader should prepare an agenda which identifies the potential problems and allows a reasonable time for informal discussion and an exchange of views. Sometimes the appointment of an independent and neutral facilitator may be able to assist in providing the right kind of atmosphere and agenda. If it is a large project of some duration, periodic meetings will assist in encouraging a co-operative outlook, particularly if there are any changes of staff at any level.

The CIB 'Best Practice Programme' includes an example of a partnership declaration in what they describe as a 'Model Project Pact'. It includes the following items:

- Deliver the project specification to the agreed budget, timetable and standards of quality.

- Adopt the CIB's Codes of Practice and Guidance where applicable and in selecting team members.

- Practise teamwork, trust, respect, fair dealing, effective communication and openness with all in the project.

- Provide all necessary skills to deliver the project.

- Build a balanced workforce.

- Seek continuous improvement with appropriate research and innovation to support the project.

- Define, manage and present the project with a responsible attitude towards the environment, the local neighbourhood and health and safety for all.

- Inform everyone involved in the project of these commitments as well as other key people within our organizations.

- Monitor performance and provide feedback to all parties during and after the project. [16]

The difficulty is to turn the *Project Pact* into a binding agreement although the ACA are exploring the possibility and hope to publish its proposals in June 2000. It will require very precise wording if it is to have any legal bite. Nevertheless, in a recent case the judge took into account the intention expressed in a partnership declaration in assessing the attitude the parties should have adopted in interpreting the contract. [17]

This was one of those cases where, following negotiations, the contractor started work on the basis of a letter of intent. A non-binding partnership charter had previously been signed between the contractor and developer in which it was stated that the parties agreed to:

produce an exceptional quality development within the agreed time frame at least cost enhancing our reputations through mutual co-operation and trust.

In due course, because of a lack of agreement on the final details, the contractor failed to sign the *JCT80* contract and subsequently withdrew from the site, maintaining that no contract existed but that they were entitled to be paid for the work already carried out. The developer countered that a contract existed and that the dispute was subject to arbitration. The Court found in favour of the developer on the grounds that, because the parties had been negotiating the terms of the contract by stages, a contract in fact existed even though a final document had not been signed. The Court further commented that the partnership charter, although non-binding, showed that the parties intended to proceed on the basis of mutual co-operation and trust which did not justify the adoption of a rigid attitude to the final details of the contract. This latter ruling was overturned by the Court of Appeal and suggests that any partnering agreement must be made binding if it has to have any legal effect.

To return to the CIB *Project Pact*, what is not specifically covered is how to overcome differences and the inevitable errors that may arise. Dealing with claims is a necessary part of the conditions of contract but, particularly in partnering, it should be seen as a procedural process to be resolved by negotiation. Any action that leads to an entrenched position should be avoided. Litigation in its various forms is not the answer. It fosters distrust, is expensive, stressful and time-consuming. How much better to accept that a problem has occurred regardless of blame and to find ways of overcoming or resolving it so that the progress of the project is not delayed and goodwill is maintained.

The original CIB Report suggests three levels of negotiation where the problem, if unresolved, is passed up the line of seniority. If the top level fails to reach agreement the dispute goes to adjudication. [18] What is missing in this hierarchy is any form of negotiation involving an independent facilitator or any process which would avoid going to the more formal procedure of adjudication which may result in the dissatisfaction of one or other of the parties and, ultimately, arbitration or litigation.

One of the elements which acts against successful partnering is the traditional manner in which site meetings are conducted and which is often used in an attempt to establish claims before the merits or otherwise have been properly assessed. It is a type of ambush that should be positively discouraged. The conduct of site meetings needs to be carefully considered and agreed upon so that only matters concerning the progress of the project are discussed and decisions made. Notes of the site meetings should be circulated and agreed. It is a good idea to number the items consecutively so that the notes become a diary of events that can be referred to easily. These should be supplemented by reference to specific documents and, where necessary, confirmed by architects' instructions.

Any cost considerations should be referred to separate meetings so that they do not impede the main purpose of the site meeting which is to progress the works. These separate meetings should be conducted in a spirit of co-operation and, if this fails to reach a resolution, the matter should be dealt with under the hierarchy formulated in the partnership charter, preferably involving a neutral facilitator. On no account should differences be allowed to fester.

At times there may be serious disagreements concerning progress and quality. Progress should be a matter of finding the best way forward and avoiding delay while deferring any cost implications to another meeting. On matters of quality, if a compromise cannot be reached the architect must make a unilateral decision. If this then leads to a question of delay or payment it becomes a cost problem that again should be discussed at a separate meeting. The primary purpose of a site meeting is to progress the works, not to argue about cost implications, even though in broad terms these may influence the decisions reached.

As yet there is little evidence of the success or otherwise of partnering despite the will to improve the present situation. Such evidence that does exist comes from large organisations where the incentive tends to be the promise of a continuing programme of work. Such agreements could fall foul of UK and EU competition legislation.

4 CAUSES OF DISPUTES

For partnering to be successful we need to understand why disputes occur and how they can be prevented. Claims for extra costs are inevitably part of the construction process and we should examine why some claims become formal disputes instead of being resolved by some form of negotiation. The types of claims at the top of the list in an American survey are variations, delays and under-certification. There are, of course, many others which I have listed in Appendix B.

Apart from those problems which can only be resolved by a legal ruling there are three main causes which prevent reasonable negotiated settlements:

1. A technical problem which is difficult to resolve either because of conflicting views or, worse still, where one party is reluctant to admit a mistake.

2. Too rigid an interpretation of the conditions of the contract.

3. Personality clashes where one or other party or both are reluctant to compromise, encouraging an element of distrust.

A conflict of views on technical problems, if allowed to escalate, may not only hold up the progress of the project but could also develop into protracted litigation involving experts on both sides. This must clearly be avoided if it is not to damage the whole operation. To do this may involve a process of negotiation, employing more than one independent technical expert whose brief should be to find a satisfactory compromise and not simply to put forward one particular solution favourable to the party he/she is representing. The selection of the technical experts to be employed could be difficult unless there is an agreement in place that permits each party to choose its own expert. An alternative on large contracts is a Disputes Review Board which will be discussed later.

The rigid interpretation of the conditions of contract is all too common and is likely to be supported in adjudication, arbitration or litigation where the tribunal has no alternative but to follow the law with no consideration of the commercial aspects or compromises which might better serve the situation. A strict interpretation of the conditions of contract should be seen only as the ultimate method of resolution where all other methods have failed.

Personality clashes are frequently brought about by entrenched attitudes held by one or more members of the combined team of client, consultant and contractor or by individuals within the same organisation, sometimes at site level. For example, a client may have delegated his powers to a member of his organisation who is reluctant to take a conciliatory attitude for fear of losing face with his employer. A site agent may not see eye-to-eye with his contract manager. Arrogance or ignorance may also play a part. An architect or engineer may insist on a particular solution to a problem when an alternative or compromise approach would be more appropriate. Every potential dispute should be approached on the basis of how best it could be resolved in the most practical and efficient way. Unless the top people in an organisation are approachable and ready to take a common sense attitude, the staff directly involved with a project will perceive that it is their duty to obtain the best possible deal for their employer even if, in the long term, a sensible compromise would best serve the project as a whole. This applies both to contractors and to clients. Co-operation between the parties should always be encouraged whether or not a formal partnership agreement exists.

Unfortunately, in most standard forms of contract there are formal notices that have to be served before claims can be pursued. This encourages the development of entrenched positions. Once notices are given they have to be answered and the tendency is for both sides to put forward the most favourable case solely in the interests of their organisation. Once made, notices are difficult to retract, thus preventing any reasonable discussion. As previously discussed, the *New Engineering Contract* includes a procedure for one or other of the parties to call an 'early warning' meeting as soon as it is apparent that any matter is likely to result in an increase in cost, a delay, or may otherwise impair the performance of the works. [19] This does not affect the legal obligations of the parties but it at least ensures that the problem will be discussed and, hopefully, resolved before the more formal claims procedure is brought into operation. If either party fails to adopt these procedures they may find themselves at a disadvantage in any subsequent litigation.

5 RECENT DEVELOPMENTS IN DISPUTE RESOLUTION

Apart from partnering there is now a change in attitude towards dispute resolution that is gradually gathering momentum.

As long ago as 1982, partly as a reaction to *JCT 80*, the Association of Consultant Architects (ACA) published its own *Form of Building Agreement*. [20] It is now in its third edition. It is only some thirty pages long, yet it is equally suitable for large and small contracts and far easier to follow than other forms. Instead of separate forms for each type of procurement it includes optional clauses for some of the alternatives within the same document. It does not cover every form of procurement but no doubt future editions will rectify this. Originally, the ACA contract included an adjudication clause which was mandatory but this was superseded by the requirements of the HGCR Act of 1996. As a result, and as a first step towards resolving differences, the latest edition includes an option for conciliation through the assistance of an independent third party. A formula such as the NEC early warning system might help to reinforce this option.

During 1987 the Federation Internationale des Ingenieurs Conseils (FIDIC) [21] introduced 'Amicable Settlement' into the fourth edition of their form of contract involving a Disputes Review Board. In 1996 this was supplemented by a form of adjudication which required the parties to give effect to the Board's decision until it was either revised or ratified by amicable settlement or by arbitration.

During 1988 the Institution of Civil Engineers (ICE) produced its first conciliation procedure.

The ADR Group was formed during 1989 comprising ADR Net, a group of some fifty firms of solicitors, and IDR Europe, which handles the referrals. This would obviously involve disputes that have already reached the litigation stage. [22]

The Centre for Dispute Resolution (CEDR), [23] founded during 1990, promotes mediation as a means of resolving disputes, including construction disputes. Its emphasis is more on resolving disputes which have reached an advanced stage.

By 1991 the Academy of Experts was already publishing guidelines for mediation.

During 1992 a group consisting mainly of civil engineers but including some architects and solicitors, set up the Construction Disputes Resolution Group (CDRG) [24] who are concerned with prevention before differences ever become disputes.

The CIC published a report in 1994 on Dispute Resolution that included a review of the various alternative methods of dispute resolution then available.[25]

During 1995 the JCT published *Practice Note 28* (see Appendix C). It is referred to in a small footnote in clause 41 which can be easily missed within an otherwise lengthy document. The Practice Note includes a brief description of the mediation process but does not set out a procedure. It includes examples of agreements for mediation, the appointment of a mediator and the terms of a settlement. It would be more helpful if the reference to mediation was included within the main body of the contract.

During 1998 the ACA published its conciliation procedure that is directly referred to in the form of contract (see Appendix D).

During 1999 the ICE published its latest conciliation procedure (see Appendix E) to be used in its family of contracts and includes a list of some fifty conciliators. It allows for the conciliator to make a recommendation if no mutual agreement is reached. [26]

Both the CIC and the Chartered Institute of Arbitrators are currently considering the formation of a panel of mediators.

6 THE WOOLF REFORMS [27]

The biggest single change is in the new 'Civil Procedure Rules' that came into force in April 1999 following Lord Woolf's Civil Justice Reforms of 1996. Under the new rules the Courts have an express duty actively to manage cases and particularly their costs. Statements of claim (now known as statements of case) will have to be far more precise and detailed at the outset. Gone are the days when vague and all embracing writs are issued merely to test the waters. Litigants may now be required to consider alternative methods of dispute resolution (ADR) and to keep costs proportional to the amount of claim.

Another innovation is that, although an expert witness has a duty to his client, his overriding duty is to the court and he is required to make a declaration to that effect. In some cases a single expert may be appointed but some lawyers fear that this may lead to complications where the instructions and documents produced by each party may conflict and the expert is given little time in which to prepare his/her report. In a recent case the court appointed a joint expert. The issues were comparatively simple but after three months the parties were not only unable to agree on the terms of the appointment but failed to provide the joint expert with the essential information he needed to prepare his report. The case at present remains unresolved.

Both the judiciary and lawyers are conservative by nature and it may be some time before the Woolf reforms are generally accepted, particularly in the regions. It is too early to evaluate the effect of these rules but it is likely that, provided the judiciary is sufficiently firm in applying them, the reforms involving closer and more accurate negotiations will become the norm and greater use will be made of alternative methods of dispute resolution.

7   ALTERNATIVE DISPUTE RESOLUTION (ADR)

The term Alternative Dispute Resolution or ADR embraces a variety of methods. All methods of dispute resolution fall within three main headings:

1. Negotiation (with or without an independent facilitator).

2. Mediation or conciliation and its variations where the procedure is conducted by an independent third party.

3. The judicial or quasi-judicial processes of adjudication, arbitration and litigation.

Alternative Dispute Resolution is a very flexible term sometimes interpreted as any form of dispute resolution other than litigation. It is more usually applied to the first two categories mentioned above.

The most elementary form of ADR is by negotiation, if necessary employing various levels as recommended in the CIB Report. Where a problem may be difficult to resolve negotiations are probably better structured under the guidance of an independent facilitator, otherwise one party may use the opportunity to obtain some psychological advantage such as deciding on the location of any meetings and the number and function of the persons to be present. Nevertheless, various forms of negotiation are widely used and are successful if the parties genuinely wish to find a satisfactory settlement, are prepared to consider an opponent's case objectively and are able to avoid entrenched positions.

Negotiations are always worth attempting even if only to narrow the issues and to arrive at a genuine attempt to try more sophisticated methods of dispute resolution without recourse to adjudication, arbitration or litigation. Whatever the circumstances, those involved in the negotiations must have powers to reach an agreement or at least be able to recommend a solution to a higher level.

The more usual form of ADR is either mediation or conciliation, which often means the same process although some organisations attach different meanings to the words. To be precise the *Oxford English Dictionary* defines 'to mediate' as the act of intervening for the purpose of reconciliation whereas 'to conciliate', although also involving reconciliation, suggests encouraging a friendly approach rather than intervention. A completely opposite interpretation has evolved whereby mediation is regarded as facilitative, aiming at a consensual solution whereas conciliation includes an element of intervention where if consensus fails, the conciliator makes a recommendation.

Thus, in current parlance mediation suggests a more relaxed approach to a dispute in which the parties genuinely wish to reach a settlement often while a contract is still in progress. Conciliation, on the other hand, has a stronger meaning in that the parties may not be so amicably disposed but nevertheless are willing to attempt to settle for commercial reasons and in order to avoid escalating costs. The conciliator in this case may take a more proactive role and is more likely to be involved when there is a stalemate.

A variation is an executive tribunal or mini trial where executives from each party take the leading role, with the mediator acting as chairman.

'Med/Arb' has nothing to do with medicine but is a hybrid term which describes the situation in which the mediator switches roles and becomes the arbitrator if a resolution is not reached by mediation.

In some contracts a disputes adviser is appointed to advise on problems as they arise with a view to avoiding formal disputes. His/her role is similar to that of a conciliator and has proved to be a very suitable arrangement for small contracts. In large contracts, as provided for by FIDIC, a Disputes Review Board is appointed consisting of a group of people, usually of different disciplines, who advise in a similar way.

In all cases in the UK where a mutually agreed settlement cannot be reached, the parties retain their statutory right to adjudication including, if necessary, the right to have the adjudicator's decision reconsidered by arbitration or by the Courts. Alternatively, an issue can be decided by expert determination, which can be final and binding.

8 CONCILIATION AND MEDIATION

With the different shades of meaning attached to these terms it will be less confusing to treat them as meaning the same thing and call the process mediation. Mediation can be defined as an attempt to resolve a dispute through negotiation with the assistance of an independent third party and which does not lead to a legally binding decision unless the parties agree that it should be so. The independent third party will need to be experienced and probably trained in the appropriate techniques which will be discussed later.

The process is not suitable where:

- The dispute concerns the interpretation of the law and a ruling is desirable in the public interest.

- The parties are so at variance that a negotiated settlement is unlikely. Even in these cases the variance may be due to misunderstandings either of the conditions of the contract or as the result of antagonism between the parties. An independent third party may be able to break the deadlock.

As one might expect ADR has a longer history in the USA where litigation is more extensive and more costly than in the UK. In a report by Douglas A. Henderson dated 1996 [28] the success of the process is discussed. In a survey quoted in the report it is apparent that mediation is most appropriate where:

- The parties wish to maintain an ongoing relationship.

- Disputes need to be resolved quickly.

- An economical process for the resolution of the dispute is desirable.

- Legal issues are likely to eclipse the commercial realities.

Some confusion exists as to the difference between 'legal issues' and 'commercial realities'. A recent dispute over fees between an architect and his client was dealt with under the *RIBA Conciliation Procedure* (see

Appendix F). The architect was proved to be legally in the right but having made his point and because he wished to maintain an otherwise satisfactory and continuing relationship, he settled for a lesser amount than he was legally entitled to. One might say that he could still have done this after obtaining an adjudicator's decision, for example, but this might have involved acrimony which both parties wished to avoid. In other cases the parties may prefer to negotiate a financial settlement simply because to establish their legal rights would involve considerable expense not only in legal fees but in time and energy. Mediation can change the whole character of a dispute. It concentrates on the parties' needs and interests, moving the focus away from their rights and liabilities. In some Asian cultures there is a profound preference for agreed solutions. They tend to seek a harmonious solution rather than one which, while factually and legally correct, may damage the relationship of the parties involved.

The procedures for mediation which are adopted by various agencies differ in detail but there are certain basic elements which are common:

- The negotiations are conducted by a neutral third party (the mediator) who establishes the rules of procedure.

- The negotiations are informal, confidential and without prejudice.

- Through discussion the mediator tries to establish the facts of the dispute to enable the parties to focus on the real issues.

- Those representing the parties must have executive authority to settle.

- The use of separate meetings (caucus sessions) between the mediator and each of the parties for the purpose of discussing in confidence matters which one party may not wish to reveal to the other and to explore the options available for settlement.

- Legal advisers may be present but only as advisers. They should not take part in the negotiations unless invited to do so on some specific point.

The procedure is normally as follows:

- Prior to any meeting there is a submission of brief written statements with supporting documents.

- A short presentation is made by each of the parties at the meeting.

- There follows a discussion of the issues with the parties both together and in private.

- The process then continues until a settlement is reached or the mediation is abandoned.

Mediations are usually of short duration and are sometimes used as a method of resolving a long-standing dispute where both parties have reached stalemate but wish somehow to break the deadlock. However, it is infinitely preferable that mediation or an intervention by a disputes adviser should take place as soon as a difference arises and before proceedings have reached this stage. Some solicitors feel that offers to mediate may appear to be a sign of weakness. It may help, therefore, if an independent third party or organisation makes the approach.

9 EXECUTIVE TRIBUNAL OR MINI TRIAL

The procedure is very similar to mediation where the executives from each party take a more active role and the mediator acts as chairman. This procedure is seldom used and omits the advantage of caucus sessions whereby each side's case can be explored confidentially.

10 MED/ARB

Some authorities take the view that because mediations are non-binding they may end up without a decision, still leaving the matter open to the more normal procedures of arbitration or litigation. In order, therefore, to avoid this lengthy process the mediator is empowered to proceed with the dispute as an arbitrator and to make an award.

The problems here are threefold:

1. Neither the parties nor the arbitrator will be able to compromise on the legal issues.

2. The parties will be reluctant during the mediation to disclose any matters of a confidential nature during caucus sessions or if they do, the mediator, when he becomes the arbitrator, may lay himself open to accusations of bias. Because of this it may even be that caucus sessions will be avoided, thus removing one of the main advantages of mediation.

3. It may be difficult in practice to decide when mediation ends and arbitration begins.

No arbitrator is going to embark upon Med/Arb without the clear consent of the parties, particularly on the question of caucus sessions. In general it mitigates against a purely commercial settlement and in some senses it is not a true mediation. In the USA the process has little support where it is considered that the mediator and the arbitrator should not be the same person. This rather defeats the objective.

11 DISPUTES ADVISER

As advocated by the Construction Disputes Resolution Group (CDRG) a disputes adviser is an independent professional consultant appointed at the beginning of a contract with the task of assisting the parties to resolve differences, claims or disputes as they arise by means of early non-binding negotiation. The appointment is usually for the duration of the contract and, depending on the details of the appointment, the disputes adviser may be required to attend administrative and site meetings and to mediate if necessary when differences occur. In small contracts it can be very helpful simply to have an agreed person on call at short notice who can give an independent opinion, advise and, if necessary, mediate on the issues involved.

12 DISPUTES REVIEW BOARD

This is a more sophisticated version of the role of the disputes adviser and is intended for very large contracts. The procedure was used for both the Channel Tunnel and Hong Kong Airport contracts. The Board consists of three or more persons, usually of different disciplines, selected by the contracting parties. It is appointed at the beginning of the contract and, by undertaking regular visits to the site, becomes part of the administration of the project while remaining independent.

The parties empower the Board to hear and advise on differences, if possible before they reach the status of disputes. The Board will then report on how it considers the matter can be resolved. As with other methods of dispute resolution it has evolved in the USA where it has been successfully used over the past twenty years and the recommendations have seldom been challenged. [29]

The powers given by the parties to the Board can vary according to agreement. Any decision can be non-binding, or binding and subject to reference to arbitration or litigation within a specific time. It can also be made legally binding although this has its dangers since the process may then bring with it the full paraphernalia associated with arbitration and litigation which is likely to be detrimental to the progress of the project. It is better that it is a temporary decision that allows the project to progress and for informal negotiations to continue for the purpose of arriving at a mutually acceptable solution.

13 EXPERT DETERMINATION

A neutral expert is appointed by the parties to decide on the dispute. His/her decision is usually binding. The expert does not have to give reasons and the decision can only be challenged if the expert has made a 'manifest error'. Most authorities agree that this is not strictly ADR since it does not allow for a settlement to be reached by negotiation and is therefore very similar to adjudication without the option of subsequent arbitration or litigation. Its main advantage is that it is quick and less costly than other methods of dispute resolution but may result in dissatisfaction of one or other of the parties.

14 STATISTICAL REVIEWS

A recent book *Dispute Resolution in the Construction Industry* [30] includes an interesting survey of the experiences of members of the construction industry, including their legal advisers. Of the various methods of ADR, negotiation and mediation were regarded as the most positive while arbitration and litigation were considered to be the least satisfactory. The traditional roles of the architect and engineer in deciding on issues had a mixed response and appear to be on the decline. However, it is apparent that where an experienced consultant is permitted to act independently the results are often satisfactory. Med/Arb, expert determination and executive tribunals seem little used. Some of those surveyed suggested that the less satisfactory aspects of adjudication might lead to a greater use of mediation.

These findings are born out by a USA survey, [31] which in considering mediation places a stress on the importance of agreeing the rules of the procedure by the parties. The agreement of the ground rules of a mediation is regarded as an essential ingredient of success as is the degree of disclosure of relevant documents. Many of those questioned in the US survey believed that contracts should require mediation before arbitration or litigation. An average success rate of sixty-five per cent is recorded for mediations and of those that lasted two or three days the success rate was as high as ninety-five per cent. This is contrary to some views held in the UK where short mediations are favoured. It is possible that longer mediations may only be relevant to construction disputes owing to their technical content and complexity. Disclosure of documents is regarded as an important factor in providing a level playing field.

15 THE PROCEDURE FOR MEDIATION

How then is mediation to be conducted?

In construction disputes it is often advisable that the mediator has a background in the industry and, ideally, first hand site experience. It is more than just understanding the rights and wrongs of the dispute, it is knowing the sort of problems and occasional misunderstandings that can arise. The USA experience (see chapter 14) supports this view.

There should be a written agreement between the parties concerning the appointment of a mediator and a date, time and place fixed. The mediator's appointment should cover the following essential points:

• The mediation is to be confidential and privileged.

• The mediator cannot be called as a witness in any subsequent litigation nor can his/her notes or opinions be used in evidence.

• The mediator shall not be liable to the parties for any act or omission whatsoever in connection with the services provided.

• The mediator's fees and expenses.

There should also be an agreement that the mediator will determine the conduct of the mediation. Nevertheless, an initial review of the ground rules is advisable in order to obtain acceptance by the parties as to how the mediation is to proceed. Often the parties and their advisers will not be familiar with the concept and time should be allowed for questions and for clarification.

As previously stated, all matters during the course of the mediation are regarded as confidential, privileged and unavailable in any future arbitration or litigation. Any restrictions will impede the success of the mediation which must be as open and as frank as possible. For the same reasons the mediator may not act as a witness in any future proceedings and must be indemnified by the parties against any liability arising from the proceedings.

Prior to the mediation it is usual for both parties to have submitted to the mediator and to each other a summary of their case together with any essential documents. The mediator must be careful not to prejudge the issues from this information. Often additional information is obtained during the mediation which is not apparent from the submitted summary.

At the meeting it is usual for the parties to present their cases verbally and be given the opportunity to cross-question each other on the conclusion of the presentations. Interruptions during the course of each presentation should not be permitted except for clarification.

The mediator should attempt to narrow the issues and obtain agreement as far as possible on the essential facts. Once this stage is completed the mediator may decide to interview the parties separately (caucus sessions) which will give him/her the opportunity to explore each case in depth and to suggest ways in which compromises might be reached. It is important that during these sessions the parties should try to recognise the merits and weaknesses of each other's case. During this process it will also be important to ascertain whether or not the parties have an interest in continuing a relationship. Several meetings of this kind may be necessary before reaching a point where the issues can again be explored mutually.

It can be an exhausting process and opportunities should be given in which the parties can relax and confer independently. Arrangements for the provision of refreshments should not be forgotten. Adjournments are helpful in avoiding fatigue and will give the parties an opportunity to reflect on the proceedings so far. The timing of the adjournments should coincide with a significant point in the mediation. If the proceedings are likely to last for more than one day, or are interrupted for any reason, it is essential to summarise in writing the stage which has been reached so that it can be reviewed at the start of the next session. In some instances the parties may not wish to continue with the mediation but later, after reflection, may decide to do so. Alternatively, the mediation may have assisted in narrowing the issues before proceeding to further litigation. For these reasons a summary of the proceedings is still important.

Finally, the mediator will attempt to persuade the parties to reach an agreement. This may require a certain amount of give and take on both sides and may lead to the realisation that a settlement is to their mutual advantage. It is essential that any agreement is perceived to be one that has been reached by the parties and not in any way imposed by the mediator unless he/she has been requested to make a recommendation as to how the dispute might be resolved. Even so, the recommendation must still be mutually acceptable.

Once a settlement is reached the mediator should draft an agreement, clearly setting out what the settlement is, what is conditional, what is binding, and any tax or other implications. It is essential that this agreement should be drafted and signed immediately on the conclusion of the mediation, even if it only covers the main heads of the agreement to be fleshed out by the parties or their legal advisers. In more complex disputes it may be that the mediator is given additional powers to adjudicate on any issues that have not already been clarified by the agreement.

As previously mentioned, the USA survey regards the disclosure of relevant documents as an important part of the success of mediations. Clearly the proceedings should not be swamped by documents and it is essential that the mediator insists that only those documents which are strictly relevant to the issues are permitted. It is necessary to distinguish between those shared between the parties and those which are not. As in arbitration and litigation there is a great temptation to include any document that is remotely relevant or used as evidence of past disagreements that have nothing to do with the case.

The mediator's fees are usually calculated on an hourly or daily basis and are shared between the parties. This should be clarified at the time of the mediator's appointment.

It should not be forgotten that the parties should ensure

that satisfactory arrangements are made for the conduct of the mediation and that there should be at least one additional room, if not two, to enable the parties to confer separately.

CHECKLIST

Before the meeting:

- Formal appointment of the mediator, including fee arrangements.
- Confidentiality of all matters.
- Date and time of meeting.
- Location of meeting and facilities to be available.
- Submission of cases plus supporting documents from both parties.
- Representatives of the parties must have authority to settle.

At the meeting:

- Introductions.
- Clarification of ground rules.
- Verbal presentation of claim and response.
- Separate meetings with the parties (caucus sessions).
- Summaries at appropriate stages.
- Written and signed statement of settlement or abandonment.

16   MEDIATION ON SMALL CONTRACTS

The procedures discussed may be too elaborate for disputes on small contracts. A simplified process may be adopted and is appropriate when neither party is sure of its legal rights. In these cases it may simply be that the parties need advice and a clarification of the issues where a disputes adviser would be more appropriate but could, if necessary, take on the role of mediator. It would be advisable to name the disputes adviser in the contract in order to avoid any disagreement when his/her services are needed. He/she should be available at the request of either party and his/her costs shared. It is particularly applicable to disputes involving residential occupiers which, as previously mentioned, are not covered by the adjudication clauses under the HGCR Act of 1996. It is important nevertheless to follow the previous checklist in principle.

17 THE TECHNIQUES OF MEDIATION

With the exception of expert determination the techniques of mediation are employed to a greater or lesser extent in all the variations of ADR, and it is important to understand that these are very different from those used in arbitration or litigation. Mediators need to acquire special skills:

- It is essential that the persons representing the parties at the mediation have the power to reach agreement. It is no good if they continually have to refer back to a higher authority.

- The mediator must be able to put the parties at their ease not only in the way that he or she conducts the proceedings but also by ensuring that the meetings are carried out in a suitably relaxed location where separate rooms are available for the parties to confer with or without the presence of the mediator. Even the arrangement of furniture can be important. A photocopier and refreshments should be available.

- The mediator's opening remarks will set the tone of the mediation. He or she should introduce him or herself, giving a brief background of qualifications and experience. The parties should also be asked to introduce themselves together with their function in both the dispute and in the proceedings.

- The mediator should then explain the ground rules, asking for questions to ensure that the rules are understood, accepted and, if necessary, modified to suit the particular dispute.

- Excessive note-taking by the mediator will be off-putting. It is better to make shorthand reminders and to rely on breaks in the proceedings to enlarge on these.

- The mediator must be a good listener and it is important not to interrupt any presentation except for the purposes of clarification.

- Eye contact is important. The parties must not feel that the mediator is aloof, disinterested or lacking in confidence.

- From time-to-time it is advisable to summarise what has been said as, very humanly, the parties may only wish to hear what suits them. At these stages the mediator should ask for questions to make sure that the summaries are understood and agreed.

- The mediator must not be discouraged if, during the first part of the proceedings, one or other or both of the parties adopt an aggressive attitude. The personal pride of individuals has a lot to do with this and personality clashes are common. The release of this aggression may be a necessary prelude to the proceedings before the real issues can be discussed dispassionately but it requires careful control. People will perceive a problem differently and often parties will adopt uncooperative stances in order to emphasise their position before being prepared to compromise.

- Body language can often be revealing as an indication of matters that one or other of the parties is not happy about. Some members may remain silent. They should be encouraged to contribute.

- The mediator should try to detect any underlying motives for the dispute or any hidden agenda.

- Separate meetings with each party (caucus sessions) are an essential part of the proceedings. Parties may be prepared to reveal in confidence matters they are not prepared to express in joint sessions. The mediator must be careful not to breach these confidences unless he/she is permitted to do so either in part or in whole.

- Part of the mediator's technique is to try to get the parties to appreciate each other's point of view. Often this has not been part of their thought process and may be one of the reasons why they have been unable to agree.

- Mediators must not allow the proceedings to be diverted by complex legal argument. If legal advisers are present they should be confined to the giving of advice only. Where parties are willing to enter into mediation they may be motivated by the desire to continue commercial relationships, provided a reasonable compromise can be reached. Legal issues may not necessarily be part of the equation. This is probably the main difference between mediation and the more formal methods of dispute resolution.

- Skill in questioning is an asset not only in assisting to clarify the issues but also in encouraging the parties to view the dispute from different angles. If the mediator anticipates the answer to his/her questions he/she must be careful not to reveal this as it may undermine his/her perceived neutrality. It may, however, be desirable in certain circumstances for the mediator to adopt a more assertive role, particularly in the caucus sessions in order to overcome what may be unreasonable attitudes.

- Above all, the mediator needs stamina in order to follow through the mediation to its conclusion, preferably without adjournment.

The role of the mediator is one of a neutral facilitator but it depends on the nature of the case and the views of the parties as to how far he or she should take a more proactive role. At one end of the scale the parties may simply be seeking advice and clarification of the issues. At the other end of the scale it may be that the parties have reached a stalemate in their negotiations or have even been directed by the Courts to undertake mediation. Whatever the circumstances the mediator should not try to coerce the parties into accepting his or her preferred outcome unless specifically requested to do so. In the end any agreement should be one which is acceptable to both parties.

18 THE USE OF SUMMARIES IN MEDIATION

These may be useful at the following stages:

• After agreement of the ground rules, especially if there is any departure from normal procedures.

• At the conclusion of the initial presentation and subsequent discussion in order to clarify the principle issues and particularly if there is any disagreement as to the detail.

• At stages where significant progress has been made towards a settlement.

• If the mediation has to be reconvened. In this case the mediator should ensure that the dates and location are suitable for all parties. It may also be opportune to obtain any further relevant documentation but if this occurs it should be circulated in advance of the next meeting.

• When no final settlement has been reached and the mediation is abandoned. It is particularly important that this should be agreed and signed since some of the issues may have been narrowed and the parties may subsequently decide to continue with negotiations.

• All summaries should be regarded as privileged and confidential.

19 THE AGREEMENT

When a settlement has been reached it is most important that it should be committed to writing immediately and signed by both the parties and by the mediator. This may take some time in order to ensure that it is precise and unambiguous. At the end of what may have been an exhausting process there will be a temptation to postpone the procedure. This must be resisted in order to avoid the parties developing different views as to what has been agreed or having second thoughts.

The agreement should include:

- The name and address of each party.

- The name of the mediator.

- The date.

- A summary of the circumstances of the mediation, its location, duration and the names of those representing the parties and their authority.

- The details of the settlement which, if necessary, can be divided into heads of agreement to be dealt with in detail by the parties' legal advisers.

- Any unresolved items, some of which the parties may wish to be mediated further or for the mediator to make recommendations.

- Any tax or VAT implications.

- Any conditions concerning actions to be carried out.

- If relevant, the discontinuation of any current legal proceedings.

- Any conditions regarding the conduct of future business relations.

- The agreement to be final and binding on the parties unless it is subject to any conditions to be fulfilled and the time limit for doing so.

- Parties reserve their rights should the settlement not be implemented.

- All matters to be treated as confidential and cannot be used in any subsequent litigation.

- The mediator to maintain his/her immunity from any liability and to be precluded from acting as a witness in any subsequent litigation.

- Signature on behalf of each party which should be dated and witnessed.

- Signature of mediator which should be dated and witnessed.

The mediation may result only in a partial agreement when a 'without prejudice' summary should be made of the proceedings and which should be dated and signed in the same way. This can be valuable in narrowing the issues in any subsequent litigation. The parties may request the mediator's recommendations. These should be 'without prejudice' and should clearly state that they do not constitute an expert determination unless specifically requested.

20 TRAINING AND SELECTION OF CONSTRUCTION MEDIATORS

Formalised training for mediators is in its infancy.

The Centre for Dispute Resolution (CEDR) runs very good residential courses for all professions. Candidates are assessed and, if successful, are accredited. To become a registered mediator one is expected to embark on a course of continuing professional development (CPD) but this does not necessarily lead to appointments and the opportunities for pupillage are few.

The Academy of Experts also runs a five-day course and maintains a register.

The ICE runs a three-day course followed by an interview. It is open to non-members. Its register is for engineers only.

IDR Net runs a course for solicitors but will also accept other professions. Its register is for solicitors only.

As the demand for mediation within the construction industry increases there are likely to be more training courses offered and various registers of those claiming to be skilled mediators. These should be treated with caution. It should also be borne in mind that many agencies are lawyer-based and are more familiar with disputes that have reached an advanced stage. Very few are involved with early dispute resolution where construction consultants with additional training are better equipped to deal with the problems. The late Judge John Newey QC is quoted as saying:

In my opinion Senior Engineers, Architects and Surveyors are ideal for providing mediators of wisdom and integrity, in whom parties can repose confidence and from whose intervention they can profit. [32]

21 AGENCIES PROVIDING MEDIATION OR CONCILIATION SERVICES

RIBA: The Royal Institute of British Architects provides a conciliation service but only involving disputes between architects and their clients. It is hoped that this will be expanded to cover all types of construction disputes (see Appendix F).

ACA: The Association of Consultant Architects includes a conciliation service within their form of building agreement. The procedure is published as a separate document that can be used independently if the parties so agree and is suitable for small contracts (see Appendix D).

CIArb: The Chartered Institute of Arbitrators is currently forming a panel of mediators.

ICE: The Institution of Civil Engineers has published a conciliation procedure (see Appendix E) and has a register of conciliators.

RICS: The Royal Institution of Chartered Surveyors maintains a list of accredited mediators. Mediators are mainly concerned with rent reviews and valuations, but some construction disputes are dealt with.

CEDR: The Centre for Dispute Resolution provides a comprehensive service more applicable to large or long-running disputes. The service is not solely for construction disputes.

CDRG: The Construction Disputes Resolution Group provides a service appropriate to any size of contract and has the advantage of being available at any stage in a difference or dispute.

CIC: The Construction Industry Council is considering providing a service.

IDR Europe (part of ADR Net): provides a comprehensive service using experienced solicitor mediators. This is more applicable to disputes that have reached an advanced stage and is not confined to construction disputes.

With the number of agencies offering a mediator service there are attempts to obtain some agreement on qualifications and possibly introducing a code of practice.

22 THE WAY FORWARD

Nobody wishes to see a continuation of the present adversarial culture that is expensive, time consuming and adds nothing to the success of a project. Sir Michael Latham in his report *Constructing the Team* lists a number of recommendations that he considers should be included in construction contracts. Although this was six years ago they are well worth repeating as they are still very relevant: [33]

1.   *A specific duty for all parties to deal fairly with each other, and with their sub-contractors, specialists and suppliers, in an atmosphere of mutual co-operation.*

2.   *Firm duties of teamwork, with shared financial motivation to pursue those objectives. These should involve a general assumption to achieve 'win-win' solutions to problems that may arise during the course of a project.*

This is very much in line with the concept of partnering although it may be difficult to incorporate as conditions within a contract except as a declaration of intent. It is more dependent on a change of culture which is already evident.

3.   *A wholly interrelated package of documents which clearly defines the roles and duties of all involved, and which is suitable for all types of project and for any procurement route.*

4.   *Easily comprehensible language with guidance notes attached.*

5.   *Separation of the roles of contract administrator, lead manager and adjudicator. The project or lead manager should be clearly defined as the client's representative.*

The reform of standard contracts along these lines is long overdue and requires some fundamental rethinking and simplification.

6.   *A choice of allocation of risks, to be decided as appropriate to each project but then allocated to*

the party best able to manage, estimate and carry the risk.

This may be difficult to achieve without including special clauses within the contract or sub-contract but it is worth considering, particularly in relation to any partnering agreement. *The New Engineering Contract* includes 'Target Contracts' as one of its options whereby the contractor shares in any savings achieved against the target figure. [34]

7. *Taking all reasonable steps to avoid changes to pre-planned works information. But, where variations do occur, they should be priced in advance, with provision for independent adjudication if agreement cannot be reached.*

Pricing variations in advance may not always be possible without disrupting the programme. Alternatively, variations should be priced within a set period and, again, subject to an independent assessment if agreement cannot be reached.

8. *Express provision for assessing interim payments by methods other than monthly valuation, i.e. milestones, activity schedules or payment schedules. Such arrangements must also be reflected in related sub-contract documentation. The eventual aim should be to phase out the traditional system of monthly measurement but meanwhile provision should still be made for it.*

9. *Clearly setting out the period within which interim payments must be made to all participants in the process, failing which they will have an automatic right to compensation, involving payment of interest at a sufficiently heavy rate to deter slow payment.*

10. *Providing for secure trust fund routes of payment.*

One of the most frequent causes of dispute is delayed or inadequate payments. The traditional system of monthly valuations is unnecessarily complex and could be replaced, as Sir Michael Latham suggests, by 'milestones' which, if not achieved in totality, could be assessed approximately and revised at the next stage payment. In simple contracts this would not be difficult but in large or complex contracts it will still be desirable to maintain a regular cash flow where some sort of valuation, albeit approximate, would be necessary. Late payment certainly requires stringent penalties.

11. While taking all reasonable steps to avoid conflict on site, providing for speedy dispute resolution if any conflict arises by a pre-determined impartial adjudicator/referee/expert.

A mediator or a disputes adviser ought to be the first port of call before statutory adjudication. Attempts have been made in standard forms of contract to achieve this but are unlikely to be wholly successful unless there is some form of partnership declaration. As matters stand at present the parties can always invoke their right to adjudication under the HGCR Act of 1996. This may require some revision in order to permit a form of prior negotiation although this might be used by the unscrupulous as a means of delaying payments.

12. Providing for incentives for exceptional performance (see 6 above).

13. Making provision where appropriate for advance mobilisation payments (if necessary bonded) to contractors and sub-contractors, including in respect of off-site prefabricated materials provided by part of the construction team.

It is not unusual in other industries for modest advance payments or deposits to be made and there is no reason why, subject to safeguards, this should not be adopted in the construction industry. There are already provisions for this but they are unrelated to the process of certification so that advance payments are treated as a loan to be repaid by the contractor by stages under a separate agreement, rather than simply being deducted from the amounts certified under the main contract. This needs a more integrated approach whereby a proportional deduction is made from each certificate valuation.

Since Sir Michael Latham made these recommendations three particular trends have emerged. The first is the movement towards a much more co-operative attitude. The second, which naturally follows, is the need for a much more sympathetic form of dispute resolution, such as the appointment of a disputes advisor or mediator. The third, which is lagging behind, is the necessity to reform standard forms of agreement so that they are less adversarial and more in line with the first two trends.

This reform of standard contracts may take some time and at present there is little evidence of this happening, although the JCT has recently set up a working party principally to review the needs of the various procurement routes now being developed. It is hoped that they will also look at ways of simplifying the forms and making them more user friendly. Meanwhile, the method by which forms of contract are selected varies considerably. An experienced client may insist on a certain form sometimes on the advice of their in-house solicitors or quantity surveyors. Too frequently, conditions of contract are amended by over zealous solicitors so that the final contents become unfamiliar. The architect or lead consultant should not be afraid to express his or her views or preferences for other forms of contract or to request that a suitable mediation clause should be included. The concept of partnering will also be unfamiliar but should be pursued.

In the case of one-off clients the architect or lead consultant may still enjoy the position of giving primary advice. Inexperienced clients may wish to take additional advice from their lawyers but one should request the opportunity to discuss the advantages and disadvantages of the various forms and of the introduction of partnering, mediation or the appointment of a disputes adviser. Many solicitors are not familiar with building contracts and the difficulties that they can lead to in practice. Before jumping on the ADR bandwagon, however, it is essential to ascertain that both parties wish to proceed down this route as the whole process might be highjacked by one of the parties insisting on adjudication if a dispute arises. There is also a danger that with court-directed mediation the legal advisers may simply see it as a hurdle to be overcome before proceeding with the familiar route of litigation. It is necessary to be on one's guard against this sort of tactic.

With the increasing interest in mediation it is apparent that two different approaches are developing. The first applies to disputes that have reached an advanced stage or have been court directed. The second and much more imaginative approach is where mediation is attempted before a difference reaches the status of a dispute. It is in this area where a disputes adviser can make a valuable contribution and should be empowered to mediate where appropriate. Experienced construction professionals with appropriate training are ideally suited to this role.

REFERENCES AND NOTES ON THE TEXT

Preface

1. Lord Donaldson: Foreword to *The ICE Arbitration Practice*, Hawker, Uff and Timms, 1983

1. Introduction

2. *Housing Grants, Construction and Regeneration Act 1996*, HMSO.

3. Institution of Civil Engineers (ICE): *New Engineering Contract*, Second Edition, Thomas Telford Publishing, 1995.

4. Association of Consultant Architects (ACA): *Form of Building Agreement 1982*, Third Edition, ACA, 1998.

5. Sir Michael Latham: *Constructing the Team*, report, HMSO, 1994.

2. Adjudication

6. *Ibid*, page 89, paragraph 9.8.

7. *Housing Grants, Construction and Regeneration Act 1996 – Part III, Section 106(2)*, HMSO.

8. Institution of Civil Engineers (ICE): *Conditions of Contract*, Sixth Edition, page 43, Section 66, Thomas Telford Publishing, 1998.

9. Institution of Civil Engineers (ICE): *New Engineering Contract*, Second Edition, clause 16, Thomas Telford Publishing, 1995

10. Centre for Dispute Resolution (CEDR): *Rules of Adjudication No. 15*.

11. Sir Michael Latham: *Constructing the Team*, page 87, paragraph 9.1: quoted from the Dispute Resolution Task Force (DART), Washington DC, February 1994.

3. Partnering

12. Construction Industry Board (CIB): *Partnering in the Team*, Working Group 12, Thomas Telford Publishing, 1997.

13. Sir John Egan, Report chaired by: *Rethinking Construction*, HMSO, 1998.

14. op cit, *Partnering in the Team*, page 3, section 2.

15. Construction Industry Council (CIC), video: *The Benefit of Hindsight*, 1999.

16. Construction Industry Board (CIB): *Construction Best Practice Programme*, 1999.

17. *Birse Construction Ltd v St David Ltd*, (1999). Appeal BLRPart II (2000), page 57.

18. op cit, *Partnering in the Team*, page 15.

4. Causes of Disputes

19. Institution of Civil Engineers (ICE): *New Engineering Contract*, Second Edition, clause 16, Thomas Telford Publishing, 1995.

5. Recent Developments in Dispute Resolution

20. Association of Consultant Architects (ACA): *Form of Building Agreement,* Third Edition, ACA 1998.

21. Federation Internationale des Ingenieurs Conseils (FIDIC), PO Box 86, 1000, Lausanne 12, Switzerland.

22. ADR Group, Grove House, Grove Road, Bristol, BS6 6UN.

23. Centre for Dispute Resolution (CEDR), Princes House, 95 Gresham Street, London, EC2V 7NA.

24. Construction Disputes Resolution Group, Early Mist, The Bridle Path, Leazes Avenue, Chaldon, Surrey, CR3 5AG.

25. Construction Industry Council (CIC): *Dispute Resolution*, 1994.

26. Institution of Civil Engineers (ICE): *Conciliation Procedure* and *List of Conciliators*, Thomas Telford Publishing, 1999.

6. The Woolf Reforms

27. Right Honourable Lord Woolf, Report by the: *Access to Justice*, HMSO, 1996.

8. Conciliation and Mediation

28. Douglas A. Henderson: *Mediation Success: An Empirical Analysis*, American Bar Association, 1996.

12. Disputes Review Board

29. *Ibid.*

14. Statistical Reviews of Dispute Resolution Methods

30. Nicholas Gould, Phillip Capper, Giles Dixon, Michael Cohen: *Dispute Resolution in the Construction Industry*, Thomas Telford Publishing, 1999.

31. *Ohio State Journal*, Vol 11.1, 1996.

20. Training and Selection of Construction Mediators

32. Peter Campbell et al: *Construction Disputes*, Whittles Publishing, Foreword, page xvii, 1997.

22. The Way Forward

33. Sir Michael Latham: *Constructing the Team*, page 37, paragraph 5.18, HMSO, 1994.

34. Institution of Civil Engineers (ICE): *New Engineering Contract*, Second Edition, optional clauses C and D, pages 32-37, Thomas Telford Publishing, 1995.

BIBLIOGRAPHY

Academy of Experts: *Guidelines for Mediation*, 1991.

Academy of Experts: *Mediation Getting Started*, 1991.

Acland, Andrew Floyer: *Resolving Disputes Without Going to Court*, Century, 1995.

Association of Consultant Architects: *ACA Conciliation Procedure*, 1998.

Association of Consultant Architects: *ACA Form of Building Agreement*, 1982, Third Edition, 1998.

Association of Consultant Architects: *Guide to ACA Form of Building Agreement*, 1999.

Blackler, Anthony: *Mediation in the New Era*, CIC Dispute Resolution Conference, October 1999.

Campbell, Peter, et al: *Construction Disputes*, Whittles Publishing, 1997.

Chartered Institute of Arbitrators: *Guidelines for Conciliation and Mediation*, 1990.

Chartered Institute of Arbitrators: Articles in 'Arbitration': *Innovation*, May 1994; *Dispute Resolution Adviser*, November 1995; *Med/Arb, ADR*, August 1996; *Changing Face of Dispute Resolution*, November 1996; *Dispute Resolution Adviser*, May 1997; *Partnering*, August 1997; *Assessing Dispute Resolution Procedures*, May 1998; *Construction Disputes*, November 1999; *Partnering*, February 2000.

Construction Industry Board: *Partnering in the Team*, Thomas Telford Publishing, 1997.

Construction Industry Board: *Construction Best Practice Programme*, Thomas Telford Publishing, 1999.

Construction Disputes Resolution Group: *Newsletter*, Autumn 1992.

Construction Disputes Resolution Group: *Amicable Dispute Settlement*, November 1993.

Construction Industry Council: *Dispute Resolution*, 1994.

Federation Internationale des Ingenieurs Conseils: *Report on Alternative Dispute Resolution*, 1992.

Gould, Nicholas: *Dispute Resolution in the Construction Industry*, Nicholas Gould, Phillip Capper, Giles Dixon, Michael Cohen, Thomas Telford Publishing, 1999.

IDR Europe Ltd: *Alternative Dispute Resolution*, Partners' Briefing Notes, 1993.

IDR Europe Ltd: *Making the Most of Mediation*, 1993.

Institution of Civil Engineers: *Conditions of Contract*, Sixth Edition, Thomas Telford Publishing, 1998.

Institution of Civil Engineers: *The New Engineering Contract*, Second Edition, Thomas Telford Publishing, 1995.

Institution of Civil Engineers: *Conciliation Procedure*, Thomas Telford Publishing, 1999.

Institution of Civil Engineers: *List of Conciliators*, Thomas Telford Publishing, 1999.

Latham, Sir Michael: *Constructing the Team*, HMSO, 1994.

Timpson, John: *The Architect in Dispute Resolution*, RIBA Publications, 1994.

Woolf, Rt Hon Lord: *Access to Justice*, HSMO, 1996.

USA

Dispute Avoidance and Resolution Task Force (DART): *Newsletter*, October 1992, Washington DC.

Henderson, Douglas A: *Mediation Success: An Empirical Analysis*, American Bar Association, 1996.

Stephenson, Ralph: *Project Partnering for the Design and Construction Industry*, Wiley Interscience, New York.

National Society of Professional Engineers, Virginia, USA: *Publication No. 1981*.

Ohio State Journal, Volume 11.1, 1996.

Schinnerer Management Services Inc: *Guidelines Volume XXII, No. 2* and *XXIII, No. 3*.

APPENDICES

APPENDIX A: JCT STANDARD FORMS OF CONTRACT

Private With Quantities

Private With Approximate Quantities

Private Without Quantities

Local Authorities With Quantities

Local Authorities With Approximate Quantities

Local Authorities Without Quantities

Contractors' Designed Portion Supplement (CDPS)

Standard Form of Building Contract with Contractor's Design (CD98)

Management Contract (MC98)

Prime Cost Contract (PCC98)

Intermediate Form of Building Contract (IFC98)

Agreement for Minor Building Works (MW98)

Various Agreements for Nominated Sub-Contractor and Suppliers

…ENDIX B: THE MAIN REASONS FOR DISPUTES

GENERAL
Adversarial conditions of contract
Rigid interpretation of contract conditions
Poor communication between parties
Proliferation of sub-contracts and warrantees not always compatible
Reluctance to pay
Distrust between parties
Incompatibility between personnel
The number of sub-contractors and suppliers
Amount of time allowed for tenders
Low tenders

CONSULTANTS
Design errors and inadequacies
Poor briefing of clients on implications of contract and building process
Delay in dealing with claims
Under certifying
Reluctance to exceed client's budget
Inexperience and lack of appropriate competence
Failure to define brief with clients
Conditions of engagement
Late or incomplete information
Poor or ambiguous specifications
Variations and late confirmation
Coordination of information
Statutory requirements

CLIENTS
Rigid budgets and poor financial arrangements
Changes of mind during construction
Poor briefing
Expectations at variance with contract documentation

Changes to standard contract conditions and additional non-standard conditions

Lack of understanding of CDM responsibilities

Interference by administrators in public authorities

Interference by clients in duties of consultants

CONTRACTOR

Inadequate site management

Poor programming

Poor workmanship

Lack of coordination of sub-contractors and suppliers

Late payment of sub-contractors

Unrealistic tenders

Deliberate pre-meditated claims and opportunist behaviour

Construction errors

SUB-CONTRACTORS AND SUPPLIERS

Terms of sub-contract mismatched with main contract

Co-ordination of design input

Failure to deliver on time

Poor performance

Failure to define performance or purpose

APPENDIX C: JCT PRACTICE NOTE 28: MEDIATION ON A BUILDING CONTRACT OR SUB-CONTRACT DISPUTE

Example A   Mediation Agreement

1   **This Agreement** made on _____ 199 ____ is between (_____)
who are the parties ("the Parties") to a building contract/sub-contract for the
carrying out of *(brief description identifying the main or sub-contract works)*.

2   The following dispute has arisen between the Parties *(set out brief
description of the dispute e.g. a valuation of a Variation, length of an
extension of time, whether the Contractor has met a performance
specification)*.

3   The Parties wish to attempt to resolve the dispute by mediation with the
assistance of *(insert name and address and qualifications)* whom they have
appointed as Mediator.

4   The mediation will commence on _____ and shall terminate

either   (a)   by agreement between the Parties on the terms of settlement
of the dispute

or   (b)   by a written notice of termination by either party to the other

or   (c)   by *(insert date)*

whichever is the earlier; provided that by further agreement the Parties may
fix a later date of termination than that stated in clause 4(c).

5   The venue for the Mediation is (_____) or such other venue as
the Parties and the Mediator may agree.

6   The conduct of the Mediation, including the extent of the documentation
required to be submitted, will be decided by the Mediator after consulting
the Parties.

7   Each party will send to the other and to the Mediator a written summary of
his case together with the supporting documentation.

8   Neither Party will in any arbitration or litigation or other proceedings on this
dispute or on any related matter call the Mediator to give evidence.

9   If a settlement is reached between the Parties it shall be set out in a written
agreement signed or executed by or on behalf of the Parties.

An example of such written agreement is given: see Example C.

10   The Mediation is to be conducted on a confidential and on a without
prejudice basis unless and until, and to the extent that, the parties otherwise
jointly agree.

Example A   *continued*

11 The fee and expenses of the Mediator will be borne by the Parties in equal shares.

12 Each party will meet its own costs incurred pursuant to the Mediation.

As witness the hands of the Parties hereto:

Signed by or on behalf of
the Employer/Contractor   _____

   in the presence of

Signed by or on behalf of
the Contractor/Sub-Contractor   _____

   in the presence of

Example B   **Agreement appointing a Mediator**

This Agreement

is made the _____ day of _____ 19 _____

BETWEEN _____
(insert names and addresses, or registered offices, of the
Employer/Contractor and Contractor/Sub-Contractor)

hereinafter called 'the Parties' or 'a Party'

AND _____
(insert the name, qualifications and address of the proposed Mediator)

hereinafter called the 'Mediator'

Whereas

the Parties have entered into an agreement (the "Mediation Agreement") in
respect of the dispute (the 'Dispute') identified in the Mediation Agreement;
and have therein stated that they wish to attempt to resolve the Dispute by
Mediation with the assistance of the Mediator;

Now it is hereby agreed that

1   The Parties and the Mediator will conduct the Mediation in accordance with
the provisions of the Mediation Agreement.

2   The Mediator will treat the Mediation as confidential and to be conducted on
a without prejudice basis between the Parties unless and until, and to the
extent that, the parties otherwise jointly agree.

3   Neither Party will in any arbitration or litigation or other proceedings on the
Dispute or any related matter call the Mediator to give evidence.

4   The Parties will be jointly and severally liable to the Mediator for his fee of

_____

and for all expenses reasonably incurred pursuant to the Mediation by the
Mediator.

continued

Example B   *continued*

As witness the hands of the Parties and of the Mediator hereto:

Signed by or on behalf of
the Employer/Contractor   _____

    in the presence of

Signed by or on behalf of
the Contractor/Sub-Contractor   _____

    in the presence of

Signed by the Mediator   _____

    in the presence of

PN 28/95

Example C   **Agreement following the resolution of a dispute after a Mediation**

This Agreement

is made the _____ day of _____ 19 _____

BETWEEN _____

_____

of/whose registered office is situated at _____

("the Employer"   "the Contractor")

AND _____

_____

of/whose registered office is situated at

("the Contractor"   "the Sub-Contractor")

Footnote [B]   pursuant and supplemental to an agreement made on _____ 19 _____

("the Building Contract", "the Sub-Contract") _____

between the Employer and the Contractor/the Contractor and the Sub-Contractor ("the Parties") for the carrying out and completion of Works ("the Works") described therein

at _____

_____

(address)

Whereas

a dispute or difference ('dispute') between the parties has arisen under the Building Contract/the Sub-Contract covering

(set out a brief summary of the dispute)

continued

Example C continued

Now it is hereby agreed

that the Parties have resolved the dispute in the following terms:

Footnote [A] 1 *(set out the terms of the settlement)*

Footnote [B] 2 The Building Contract/Sub-Contract shall have effect subject to the terms of settlement set out in clause 1 which are from the date hereof incorporated into and form part of the Building Contract/Sub-Contract.

Footnote [B] 3 If there is any conflict between the terms of the Building Contract/the Sub-Contract and the terms of settlement set out in clause 1 those terms of settlement shall prevail.

Footnote [B] Attestation

Footnotes

[A] In drafting clause 1 consideration should be given to the effect of the agreed terms on any related contracts, sub-contracts, warranties etc.

[B] Where the Agreement does not simply resolve a past dispute but affects or may affect the future operation of the Building Contract/Sub-Contract it is necessary that the Agreement is a supplemental agreement to the Building Contract/Sub-Contract and includes words of similar effect to those in clauses 2 and 3; and is executed under hand or as a deed as the Building Contract/Sub-Contract.

PN 28/95

Appendix D: ACA Conciliation Procedure

THE ASSOCIATION OF CONSULTANT ARCHITECTS

CONCILIATION PROCEDURE 1998

1.00   INTRODUCTORY NOTES

1.01   Conciliation is available for parties to an ACA Contract (ACA refers herein to The Association of Consultant Architects) in which an Architect is either a party to that contract or who is acting on behalf of one of the parties to that contract.

1.02   Conciliation is an alternative to Adjudication, Litigation or Arbitration and is a first step procedure to resolving any dispute or difference. It is an informal and confidential process which does not impose on the parties a resolution to a dispute unless mutually acceptable. Instead it allows the parties the freedom to explore ways of settling the dispute with the assistance of an impartial and independent person (the Conciliator). Being confidential, nothing said during the process can be used at a later date in any form of legal proceedings. Furthermore, information given to the Conciliator in confidence by Party A cannot be disclosed to Party B without the express permission of Party A and vice versa.

1.03   The Conciliator will attempt to define and if possible narrow the issues. If requested to do so by the parties, he may assist in proposing a resolution as to how the dispute or difference might be settled. Conciliation is essentially a process in which the Conciliator assists in negotiations between the parties to arrive at a binding settlement which they consider to be mutually and commercially acceptable.

1.04   Evidence is not given under oath nor affirmation. The Conciliator is not bound by the rules of the Courts or of natural justice and can only be guided by what the parties choose to tell him and by his own professional knowledge and experience.

1.05   Conciliation is only suitable where the parties have a genuine wish to settle. It is not suitable where the parties are seeking to resolve a dispute solely on the basis of their legal rights.

1.06   Conciliators are selected from ACA members approved by the President of the ACA for appointment under the scheme.

1.07   In selecting a location for the Conciliation facilities should be available for the parties to confer separately.

1.08   Those wishing to take advantage of the scheme should apply to the Secretary General of the ACA at 98 Hayes Road, Bromley, Kent BR2 9AB   Tel: 0181 325 1402   Fax: 0181 883 2226).

2.00   THE ACA CONCILIATION PROCEDURE RULES AND CONDITIONS

Where the context so requires 'party' shall mean 'parties' and 'he' shall mean 'she'.

PRELIMINARIES

2.01   The Scheme is administered by the Secretary General of the ACA. Parties wishing to apply for conciliation under the Scheme will apply jointly to the Secretary General of the ACA setting out in concise terms the nature of the difference or dispute.   The application should be accompanied by the prescribed administrative fee.

2.02   When the Secretary General is satisfied that both parties have agreed to the ACA Conciliation Procedure, (hereinafter called 'the Procedure') and that the dispute or difference is suitable for conciliation, the President of the ACA will appoint a Conciliator who will proceed with the case with a minimum of delay upon the signing of the Conciliator's Agreement and the payment of the Conciliator's preliminary fee.

COSTS

2.03   Costs will be as follows and subject to adjustment from time to time:

Registration charge upon making the application: £25.00 from each of the parties (total £50.00).

Conciliator's charges: £............. per day or part of a day. Charges for the first day are payable in advance.

In addition the Conciliator is entitled to charge for his time in reading documentation together with time and expenses for travelling, subsistence, telephone, fax, e-mail, photocopying and postal charges.

All charges and expenses will be subject to VAT where applicable. The parties shall be jointly and severally responsible for the payment of the charges and expenses and will normally be expected to share them equally. Each party will be responsible for its own costs.

PROCEDURE

2.04   Prior to the Conciliation all parties will have submitted to the Conciliator and will have exchanged copies of written summaries of their cases and any relevant documentation together with the names of their representatives and any advisers who will attend the Conciliation.

2.05   The representatives of the Parties at the Conciliation must have full authority to settle the dispute or difference.

2.06   The Conciliation will take place on a day and at a location to be agreed between the Parties and the Conciliator and such additional days as shall be agreed.

2.07   The procedure at the Conciliation shall be determined by the Conciliator and may include the submission of additional evidence whether documentary or oral and site inspections. The Conciliator may also require to meet the parties separately. In such circumstances the Conciliator may not disclose to the other party any information given to him without consent.

2.08   The Conciliator may obtain legal and/or technical advice with the consent of the parties.

THE CONCLUSION OF THE CONCILIATION

2.09   If at the conclusion of the Conciliation a settlement is reached between the Parties, the terms of the settlement will be set down in writing and signed by the Parties. The Parties will undertake to give effect to such settlement forthwith in accordance with its terms. Copies of the agreement will be retained by each of the parties, the Conciliator and the Secretary General of the ACA.

2.10   If a settlement is not reached or one of the Parties withdraws, or in the opinion of the Conciliator is unlikely to be achieved, this shall be confirmed in writing by the Conciliator and the conciliation abandoned.

2.11   All Parties reserve their respective rights should a settlement not be reached.

CONFIDENTIALITY AND IMMUNITY

2.12   The Parties and the Conciliator undertake to each other and agree that:

i.   the entire conciliation procedure will be kept confidential.

ii.   the Parties, their representatives and advisers and the Conciliator shall keep confidential all statements and all other matters whether written or oral including any settlement agreement relating to the Conciliation except insofar as disclosure is necessary to implement and enforce the settlement agreement.

iii.   the process of the Conciliation shall be treated on a without prejudice basis. All submissions and statements whether written or oral and produced for the purposes of the Conciliation shall be in admissible and not subject to discovery in any subsequent proceedings. Evidence which is otherwise admissible or discoverable will not be subject to this exclusion. The Parties shall not have access to any notes made by the Conciliator during the course of the proceedings.

2.13   The Conciliator shall not be required to act as an Adjudicator or Arbitrator in any subsequent proceedings nor shall he be called as a witness in any subsequent proceedings.

2.14   The Parties also agree that neither the ACA nor the Conciliator nor their agents or employees shall be liable for anything done or omitted in the discharge or purported discharge of their functions.

THE CONCILIATOR'S AGREEMENT

This AGREEMENT is made on the . . . . .day of . . . . .19 . . . . .

Between . . . .(first party)

of . . . .

and . . . .(second party)

of . . . .

and (where there is a third party) . . . .

of . . . .

(hereinafter called 'the Parties') of the one part

and . . . .

of . . . .

(hereinafter called 'the Conciliator') of the other part.

A dispute or difference having arisen between the Parties in connection with

. . . .

. . . .

The Parties have agreed that the dispute or difference shall be considered under the Rules and Conditions of the ACA Conciliation Procedure (1998) and have agreed to the appointment of the Conciliator and have asked him to act under the Rules and Conditions of the Procedure.

This agreement shall be governed by and construed in accordance with English law under the jurisdiction of the English Courts.

IT IS NOW AGREED as follows:-

(i)   The Conciliator hereby accepts the appointment and agrees to conduct the Conciliation in accordance with the said Procedure.

(ii) The Conciliator shall be paid at the rate of £. . . . . .per day or part of a day during the course of the Conciliation. An amount of £. . . . . will become due upon the signing of this agreement.

(iii) The Conciliator shall be reimbursed in respect of all disbursements properly incurred in connection with the Conciliation.

(iv) The Parties will be jointly and severally responsible for the payment of the costs and disbursements.

SIGNED

First Party . . . .

on behalf of . . . .

. . . .

Witness: . . . .

Third Party

(where applicable) . . . .

on behalf of: . . . .

. . . .

Witness . . . .

Second Party . . . .

on behalf of: . . . .

. . . .

Witness . . . .

The Conciliator . . . .

Witness . . . .

APPENDIX E: ICE CONCILIATION PROCEDURE

THE INSTITUTION OF CIVIL ENGINEERS' CONCILIATION PROCEDURE (1999)

1.   GENERAL PRINCIPLES

1.1   This Procedure shall apply whenever: the Parties have entered into a contract which provides for conciliation for any dispute which may arise between the Parties in accordance with The Institution of Civil Engineers' Conciliation Procedure, or where the Parties have agreed that The Institution of Civil Engineers' Conciliation Procedure shall apply.

1.2   The conciliation shall be conducted in accordance with the edition of the ICE Conciliation Procedure which is in force at the date of issue of the Notice of Conciliation.

1.3   This Procedure shall be interpreted and applied in the manner most conducive to the efficient conduct of the proceedings with the primary objective of achieving a settlement to the dispute by agreement between the Parties as quickly as possible.

2.   THE NOTICE OF CONCILIATION

2.1   Subject to the provisions of the contract relating to conciliation, any Party to the contract may by giving to the other Party a written notice, hereinafter called a Notice of Conciliation, request that any dispute in connection with or arising out of the contract or the carrying out of the Works shall be referred to a Conciliator. Such Notice shall be accompanied by a brief statement of the matter or matters which it is desired to refer to conciliation, and the relief or remedy sought.

3.   THE APPOINTMENT OF THE CONCILIATOR

3.1   Save where a Conciliator has already been appointed, the Parties shall agree upon a Conciliator within 14 days of the Notice being given under paragraph 2.1. In default of agreement any Party may request the President (or, if he is unable to act, any Vice President) for the time being of the Institution of Civil Engineers to appoint a Conciliator within 14 days of receipt of the request by him, which request shall be accompanied by a copy of the Notice of Conciliation.

3.2   If, for any reason whatsoever, the Conciliator is unable, or fails to complete the conciliation in accordance with this Procedure, then any Party may require the appointment of a replacement Conciliator in accordance with paragraph 3.1.

4. CONDUCT OF THE CONCILIATION

4.1 Unless otherwise agreed by the Parties, the Party requesting conciliation shall deliver to the Conciliator, immediately on his appointment, with a copy to the other Party, a copy of the Notice of Conciliation together with copies of all relevant Notices of Dispute and of any other notice or decision which is a condition precedent to conciliation.

4.2 The Conciliator shall start the conciliation as soon as possible after his appointment and shall use his best endeavours to conclude the conciliation as soon as possible and in any event within any time limit stated in the contract, or two months from the date of his appointment whichever is the earlier, or within such other time agreed between the Parties.

4.3 Any Party may, upon receipt of notice of the appointment of the Conciliator and within such period as the Conciliator may allow, send to the Conciliator and to the other Party a statement of its views on the dispute and any issues that it considers to be of relevance to the dispute, and any financial consequences.

4.4 As soon as possible after his appointment, the Conciliator shall issue instructions establishing, amongst other things, the date and place for the conciliation meeting with the Parties. Each Party shall, in advance of the meeting, inform the Conciliator, and the other Party, in writing of the name of its representative for the conciliation, who shall have full authority to act on behalf of that Party and the names of any other persons who will attend the conciliation meeting.

4.5 The Conciliator may:
   (a) issue such further instructions as he considers to be appropriate;
   (b) meet and question the Parties and their representatives, together or separately;
   (c) investigate the facts and circumstances of the dispute;
   (d) visit the site;
   (e) request the production of documents or the attendance of people whom he considers could assist in any way.

4.6 The Conciliator may conduct the proceedings in any way that he wishes, and with the prior agreement of the Parties obtain legal or technical advice, the cost of which shall be met by the Parties, in accordance with paragraph 5.4, or as agreed by the Parties and the Conciliator.

4.7 The Conciliator may consider and discuss such solutions to the dispute as he thinks appropriate or as suggested by any Party. He shall observe and maintain the confidentiality of particular information which he is given by any Party privately, and may only disclose it with the express permission of that Party. He will try to assist the Parties to resolve the dispute in any way which is acceptable to them.

4.8 Any Party may, at any time, ask that additional claims or disputes, or additional Parties, shall be joined in the conciliation. Such requests shall be accompanied by details of the relevant contractual facts, notices and decisions. Such joinder shall be subject to the agreement of the Conciliator and all other Parties. Any additional Party shall, unless otherwise agreed by the Parties, have the same rights and obligations as the other Parties to the conciliation.

4.9 If, in the opinion of the Conciliator, the resolution of the dispute would be assisted by further investigation by any Party or by the Conciliator, or by an interim agreement, including some action by any Party, then the Conciliator will, with the agreement of the Parties, give instructions and adjourn the proceedings as may be appropriate.

4.10 When a settlement has been achieved of the whole or any part of the matters in dispute the Conciliator shall, if so requested by all the Parties, assist them to prepare an Agreement incorporating the terms of the settlement. If requested in writing by all the Parties, the Conciliator may be appointed by the Parties as an arbitrator with authority solely to issue a consent award.

5.   THE RECOMMENDATION

5.1 The Conciliator shall advise all Parties accordingly and prepare his recommendation forthwith:
    (a)   if in the opinion of the Conciliator it is unlikely that the Parties will agree a settlement to their disputes, or
    (b)   if any Party fails to respond to an instruction by the Conciliator, or
    (c)   if requested by any Party.

5.2 The Conciliator's recommendation shall state his solution to the dispute which has been referred for conciliation. The recommendation shall not disclose any information which any Party has provided in confidence. It shall be based on his opinion as to how the Parties can best dispose of the dispute between them and need not necessarily be based on any principles of the contract, law or equity.

5.3   The Conciliator shall not be required to give reasons for his recommendation.

5.4   When a settlement has been reached or when the Conciliator has prepared his recommendation, or at an earlier date solely at the discretion of the Conciliator, he shall notify the Parties in writing and send them an account of his fees and disbursements. Unless otherwise agreed between themselves each Party shall be responsible for paying and shall within 7 days of receipt of the account from the Conciliator pay an equal share save that the Parties shall be jointly and severally liable to the Conciliator for the whole of his account. If any Party fails to make the payment due from him, the other Party may pay the sum to the Conciliator and recover the amount from the defaulting Party as a debt due. Each Party shall meet his own costs and expenses. Upon receipt of payment in full the Conciliator shall send his recommendation to all the Parties.

5.5   The Conciliator may be recalled, by written agreement of the Parties and upon payment of an additional fee, to clarify, amplify or give further consideration to any provision of the recommendation.

6.   MISCELLANEOUS PROVISIONS

6.1   No Party shall be entitled to call the Conciliator as a witness in any subsequent adjudication, arbitration or litigation concerning the subject matter of the conciliation.

6.2   The Conciliator shall not be appointed adjudicator in any subsequent adjudication, or arbitrator (except as provided for in paragraph 4.10) in any subsequent arbitration between the Parties whether arising out of the dispute, difference or other matter or otherwise arising out of the same contract unless the Parties otherwise agree in writing.

6.3   The Parties and the Conciliator shall at all times maintain the confidentiality of the conciliation and shall endeavour to ensure that anyone acting on their behalf or through them will do likewise.

6.4   The Conciliator shall not be liable to the Parties or any person claiming through them for any matter arising out of or in connection with the conciliation or the way in which it is or has been conducted, and the Parties shall not themselves bring any such claims against him.

6.5   Any notice required under this Procedure shall be sent to the Parties by recorded delivery to the principal place of business or if a company to its registered office, or to the address which the Party has notified to the Conciliator. Any notice required by this Procedure to be sent to the Conciliator shall be sent by recorded delivery to him at the address which he shall notify to the Parties on his appointment.

6.6   In this Procedure where the context so requires 'Party' shall mean 'Parties' and 'he' shall mean 'she'.

CONCILIATOR'S AGREEMENT

THIS AGREEMENT is made on . . . . . . .day of . . . . .year . . . .
between (the first Party)
of:

and (the second Party)
of:

and (the third Party if any)
of:

(hereinafter called 'the Parties') of the one part and
of:

(hereinafter called 'the Conciliator') of the other part.
Disputes or differences have arisen between the Parties in connection with
certain construction works known as:

. . . .

. . . .

and the Parties have agreed that these disputes or differences shall be
considered under the Institution of Civil Engineers' Conciliation Procedure
(1999) (hereinafter called 'the Procedure') and have agreed to ask the
Conciliator to act.

IT IS NOW AGREED as follows:

1. The rights and obligations of the Conciliator and the Parties shall be as
    set out in the Procedure.
2. The Conciliator hereby accepts the appointment and agrees to conduct
    the conciliation in accordance with the Procedure.
3. The Parties bind themselves jointly and severally to pay the
    Conciliator's fees and expenses in accordance with paragraph 5.4 of
    the Procedure in the manner set out in the attached Schedule.

Signed on behalf of:
First Party:

Name:

Signature:

Date:

Second Party:

Name:

Signature:

Date:

Third Party (if any):

Name:

Signature:

Date:

Conciliator:

Name:

Signature:

Date:

SCHEDULE TO THE CONCILIATOR'S AGREEMENT

1.   The Conciliator shall be paid at the hourly rate of £   in respect of all time spent upon, or in connection with, the conciliation including time spent travelling.

2.   The Conciliator shall be reimbursed in respect of all disbursements properly made including, but not restricted to:

    (a)   Printing, reproduction and purchase of all documents, drawings, maps, records and photographs.

    (b)   Telegrams, telex, faxes and telephone calls.

    (c)   Postage and similar delivery charges.

    (d)   Travelling, hotel expenses and other similar disbursements.

    (e)   Room charges.

    (f)   Charges for legal or technical advice obtained in accordance with the Procedure.

3.   The Conciliator shall be paid an appointment fee of £   . This fee shall become payable in equal amounts by each Party within 14 days of the appointment of the Conciliator. This fee will be deducted from the final statement of any sums which shall become payable under Item 1 and/or Item 2 of this Schedule. If the final statement is less than the appointment fee the balance shall be refunded to the Parties.

4.   The Conciliator is/is not* currently registered for VAT.

5.   When the Conciliator is registered for VAT, VAT shall be charged additionally in accordance with the rates current at the date of invoice.

6.   All payments, other than the appointment fee (Item 3) shall become due 7 days after receipt of invoice, thereafter interest shall be payable at 10% per annum above the Bank of England base rate for every day the amount remains outstanding.

*Delete as necessary

Notice to Refer a Dispute to Conciliation

To: *(Name of Responding Party)*
        (Address of Responding Party)

Date:

NOTICE OF CONCILIATION
(Reference   )

(Contract Name:)

We consider that the following dispute(s) or difference(s) have arisen between us:

We now give notice that we request these dispute(s) or difference(s) to be referred to conciliation and the relief/remedy being sought is:

Yours faithfully

For and on behalf of
(Referring Party)

APPENDIX F: RIBA CONCILIATION PROCEDURE

INTRODUCTION

1. Conciliation is an alternative to adjudication, arbitration and litigation. It is an informal process, which does not impose a resolution to a dispute and only becomes binding with the consent of each of the parties. Conciliation allows the parties the freedom to explore ways of settling the dispute with the assistance of an impartial and independent person (the Conciliator). It is essentially a process in which the Conciliator assists in negotiations between the parties to arrive at a settlement.

2. The overall intention of Conciliation is to reach an agreed solution. If that proves to be impossible then the Conciliator will attempt to narrow the issues and, if requested to do so by the parties, will make a recommendation as to how the dispute might be settled. The recommendation is in no way binding unless the parties wish it to be so.

3. The proceedings are conducted on a privileged and 'without prejudice' basis. Nothing disclosed during the conciliation process can be used as evidence in any subsequent proceedings whether adjudication, arbitration or litigation. Nor can the Conciliator be appointed as adjudicator or arbitrator or called as a witness in any subsequent proceedings.

4. The information given to the Conciliator may not necessarily be comprehensive. It is not given under oath nor affirmation; nor is there any cross-examination. The Conciliator is not bound by the rules of natural justice or by the rules of evidence and can be guided only by what the parties choose to tell him and by his own professional knowledge and experience.

   In the event of the parties requesting a recommended settlement from the Conciliator it follows that, because the information given to him may be selective, a recommendation is in no way comparable to the decision of an adjudicator, an award by an arbitrator, or a court judgment.

5. A recommendation represents the opinion of the conciliator of how in his judgment the dispute might be settled in the most practical way.

PROCEDURE

1.   Under the Scheme conciliation is offered as an alternative means of dispute resolution (ADR) where differences or disputes arise between members of the RIBA and their clients, between an employer and a contractor, between a contractor and sub-contractor or between members of the RIBA. It is only suitable where the parties have a genuine wish to settle. Conciliators are selected from RIBA members who have been approved by the National Practice Committee or a Regional Council of the RIBA for appointment under the Scheme. In this procedure where the context so requires 'party' shall mean 'parties' and 'he' shall mean 'she'.

2.   Unless requested to do so by the parties the Conciliator will not make a recommendation for settlement but will attempt to bring the parties to a settlement by discussing the differences with the parties separately or together and advising on the strengths and weaknesses of their respective cases. The proceedings will be conducted in confidence and on a without prejudice basis and nothing disclosed in confidence to the Conciliator by either party shall be conveyed to the other party unless it is agreed that he should do so.

3.   The scheme is not available for resolution of disputes where:
   a)   adjudication, arbitration or litigation is already in progress unless the parties agree to suspend the proceedings while conciliation takes place;
   b)   a party is seeking to resolve a dispute on a question of law.

4.   The Scheme is co-ordinated centrally by a member of RIBA HQ staff reporting to the director of Practice and administered regionally by RIBA regional staff. Parties wishing to apply for conciliation under the Scheme will apply jointly or individually to the Administrator setting out in concise terms the nature of the difference or dispute.

   When the Administrator is satisfied that both parties agree to the procedure and that the dispute or difference is suitable for conciliation he will, on receipt of the application fee, nominate a Conciliator who will proceed with the case with a minimum of delay upon the signing of the Conciliators Agreement.

   If a settlement is reached the parties will be required to sign an agreement which, if agreed, can be binding. The contents of the agreement will be confidential. Copies will be retained by the parties, the Conciliator and the Administrator.

5.   A conciliation may be abandoned at any time by the withdrawal of one of the parties or if the Conciliator is of the opinion that no useful purpose can be achieved by continuing.

6.   Neither the RIBA nor the Conciliator shall be liable for anything done or omitted in the discharge or purported discharge of their functions and any employee or agent of the Conciliator is similarly protected from liability.

THE CONCILIATOR'S AGREEMENT

This AGREEMENT

is made on . . . . day of . . . .(month) . . . . (year)

BETWEEN

. . . .(first party)

of . . . .

. . . .

AND

. . . .(second party)

of . . . .

. . . .

(Where there is a third party)

AND

of . . . .

(hereinafter called 'the Parties') of the one part

AND

of . . . .

(hereinafter called 'the Conciliator') of the other part.

A dispute or differences having arisen between the Parties in connection with:

. . . .

. . . .

and the Parties have agreed that the disputes or differences shall be considered under the RIBA Conciliation Procedure (1998) (hereinafter called 'the Procedure') and have agreed to the appointment of the Conciliator and have asked him to act under the Conditions.

CONDITIONS

1. Prior to the Agreement both Parties will have submitted to the Conciliator and will have exchanged copies of a written summary of their case and any relevant documentation.

2. The representatives of the Parties at the Conciliation will have full authority to settle the disputes or differences.

3. The Conciliation will take place on a day to be agreed between the Parties and the Conciliator and such additional days as shall be agreed.

4. The Conciliator shall determine the procedure at the Conciliation.

5. The Conciliation will continue during the day(s) agreed until a either a settlement is reached, or one of the Parties withdraws, or in the opinion of the Conciliator a settlement is unlikely to be achieved.

6. If the Parties require and the Conciliator agrees he will make recommendations as to the terms of the settlement. This will not constitute an attempt to anticipate either an adjudicator's decision, an arbitrator's award or a court order.

7. If at the conclusion of the Conciliation a settlement is reached between the Parties, Heads of Agreement will be prepared and signed by the Parties and endorsed by the Conciliator, but shall not be binding unless the Parties so agree. If it is agreed that the settlement shall be binding then the Parties will be legally bound by the settlement and will undertake to give effect to such settlement forthwith in accordance with its terms.

8. All Parties reserve their respective rights should a settlement not be reached.

9. The Parties undertake to each other and agree that:

    (i) the entire conciliation procedure is and will be kept confidential;

    (ii) the Parties, their representatives and advisers and the Conciliator shall keep confidential all statements and all other matters whether written or oral including any settlement agreement relating to the conciliation except insofar as disclosure is necessary to implement and enforce the settlement agreement;

    (iii) the process of the conciliation shall be treated as privileged and without prejudice. All submissions and statements whether written or oral and produced for the purposes of the Conciliation shall be inadmissible and not subject to discovery in any subsequent proceedings except that evidence which is otherwise admissible or discoverable shall not become inadmissible or non-discoverable by reason of its use in the Conciliation. The Parties shall not have access to any notes made by the Conciliator during the course of the proceedings.

10. The Conciliator shall not be required to act as an Adjudicator or Arbitrator in any subsequent proceedings nor shall he be called as a witness in any subsequent proceedings.

11. The Parties agree that neither the RIBA nor the Conciliator nor their agents or employees shall be liable for anything done or omitted in the discharge or purported discharge of their functions.

12. This agreement shall be governed by and construed in accordance with law of England and Wales under the jurisdiction of the English Courts.

13. (i) The Conciliator shall be paid at the rate of £. . . .per day or part of a day during the course of the Conciliation.

    (ii) An amount of £. . . . will become due upon the signing of this agreement.

    (iii) The Conciliator shall be reimbursed in respect of all disbursements properly incurred in connection with the Conciliation.

    (iv) The Conciliator is/is not registered for VAT. Chargeable VAT shall be added to the fee and expenses as applicable.

The Parties will be jointly or severally responsible for the payment of the fees and disbursements.

SIGNED on behalf of   in the presence of

. . . .*(first party)*   . . . .

and

. . . . *(second party)*

and

(Where there is a third party)

. . . .

and

. . . . *(Conciliator)*   . . . .

APPENDIX G: USEFUL ADDRESSES

Association of Consultant Architects (ACA): 98 Hayes Road, Bromley, Kent, BR2 9AB (t) 020 8325 1402 (f) 020 8883 2226.

Academy of Experts: 116-118 Chancery Lane, London, WC2A 1PP (t) 020 7637 0333 (f) 020 7637 1893.

ADR Net: Grove House, Grove Road, Redland, Bristol, BS6 6UN (t) 0117 946 7180 (f) 0117 946 7181.

Centre for Dispute Resolution (CEDR): Princes House, 95 Gresham Street, London, EC2V 7NA (t) 020 7600 0500 (f) 020 7600 0501.

Construction Disputes Resolution Group (CDRG): Early Mist, The Bridle Path, Leazes Avenue, Chaldon, Surrey, CR3 5AG (t/f) 01883 623 801.

Construction Industry Board (CIB): 26 Store Street, London, WC1E 7BT (t) 020 7636 2256 (f) 020 7637 2258.

Construction Industry Council (CIC): 26 Store Street, London, WC1E 7BT (t) 020 7637 8692 (f) 020 7580 6140.

Chartered Institute of Arbitrators, International Arbitration Centre (CIArb): 24 Angel Gate, City Road, London, EC1V 2RS (t) 020 7837 4483 (f) 020 7837 4285.

Institution of Civil Engineers (ICE): 1 Great George Street, London, SW1P 3AA (t) 020 7222 7722 (f) 020 7222 1403.

RICS Dispute Resolution Service: Surveyor Court, Westwood Way, Coventry, CV4 8JE (t) 024 7669 4757 (f) 020 7334 3802